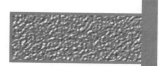

Children
Who Lose
Their Parents
to HIV/AIDS

Agency Guidelines
for Adoptive and
Kinship Placement

D1314074

by Lisa Merkel-Holguín

Child Welfare League of America
Washington, DC

CWLA Press
an imprint of the Child Welfare League of America, Inc.

CHILD WELFARE LEAGUE OF AMERICA, INC.
440 First Street, NW, Suite 310, Washington, DC 20001-2085

CURRENT PRINTING (last digit)
10 9 8 7 6 5 4 3 2 1

Cover design by Kerri Washington for Alexhon
Text design by Kerri Washington for Alexhon

Printed in the United States of America

ISBN # 0–87868–631–2

Library of Congress Cataloging-in-Publication Data

CONTENTS

■ ■ ■ ■ ■

ACKNOWLEDGMENTS

■ ■ ■ ■ ■

The Child Welfare League of America (CWLA) is pleased to acknowledge the dedication and helpfulness of many people in developing these guidelines. First, these guidelines would not have been possible without the generous financial support of the Prudential Foundation. CWLA appreciates the vision and commitment of the Prudential Foundation in recognizing the burgeoning need in the child welfare field to create programs, policies, and practices that help agencies place children who lose their parents to AIDS with adoptive and extended families.

CWLA also acknowledges the leadership of the CWLA National Task Force on Children and HIV Infection and its Subcommittee for their guidance in developing this workbook. The Task Force's Subcommittee met four times over an 18-month period to conceptualize policy and program tenets that were incorporated into these guidelines to help child welfare agencies serving HIV-affected families.

Terry Zealand, Chair of the Subcommittee to Place Children Who Lose Their Parents to AIDS with Extended and Adoptive Families and Executive Director of the AIDS Resource Foundation for Children (ARFC), provided skillful leadership and unquestioning commitment. Donna Pressma, Chair of the National Task Force and Executive Director of the Children's Home Society of New Jersey, demonstrated her longstanding commitment to children and families affected by HIV/AIDS. The Task Force Subcommittee members, who deserve our gratitude for giving so generously of their time in reviewing drafts and providing suggestions, are noted in Appendix A.

Many CWLA associates also contributed to the development of these guidelines and are deserving of thanks: Madelyn DeWoody, former Director of Child Welfare Services and General Counsel, and Ann Sullivan, Adoption Program Director for their steadfast guidance, suggestions, support, and conceptualization of the project; Cynthia Beatty, CWLA General Counsel, for her analysis of standby guardianship legislation; Bronwyn Mayden, CWLA Program Director for Adolescent Parenting and Pregnancy Prevention, for her supervision of this project; Bonnie Kerker, 1994 Everett Public Service Intern, for her assistance in reviewing and drafting parts of this document; and Peter Slavin for his editing expertise.

As the HIV/AIDS pandemic continues to spread, every individual, family, and community is affected: homosexual, heterosexual, Caucasian, African American, Latino, male, and female. HIV/AIDS knows no boundaries. Currently, in the United States, heterosexual transmission is significantly increasing, particularly among certain racial and ethnic populations as well as adolescent and young adult subgroups.

Across the United States and the world, children who lose their parents to HIV/AIDS are one of the fastest emerging groups affected by this epidemic. Yet, they are also the least known group, receive the least service, and pose serious issues for the child welfare system now and in the foreseeable future. Because these emerging populations are groups often served by the child welfare community, child welfare agencies must work to develop innovative services. Although the majority of children who lose their parents to HIV/AIDS are healthy in the sense that they are not HIV infected, they, like children who are HIV positive, have a common need—someone to care for them.

Increasingly, child welfare and family service agencies are providing services to parents who are HIV infected and helping them to secure legal and permanent care arrangements for their children. Many children who lose their parents to HIV/AIDS, however, are unnecessarily entering an already overburdened foster care system. Others are living with kin who are overextended and who may not have the capacity to adequately care for them. When parents who are HIV positive receive help in developing formal, legal, and permanent plans, their children are more likely able to move to new adoptive families or to extended family members who are prepared and who have adequate resources to care for them, before or upon the death of the children's parent(s).

This document, *Children Who Lose Their Parents to AIDS: Agency Guidelines for Adoptive and Kinship Placement*, builds on the prior, groundbreaking work of the National Task Force on Children and HIV Infection of the Child Welfare League of America (CWLA). Over a three-year span (1989 to 1991), the Task Force and its Subcommittees developed three sets of guidelines: *Meeting the Challenge of HIV Infection in Family Foster Care; Serving HIV-Infected Children, Youth and Their Families: A Guide for Residential Group Care Providers; and Serving Children with HIV Infection in Child Day Care*. These guidelines have assisted child welfare agencies to care for children and adolescents who are HIV infected and have prompted many child welfare agencies to develop policies and procedures to ensure that children, young people, and their families are served compassionately and competently in various child welfare settings. In addition, CWLA published a *Report of the Task Force on Children and AIDS: Initial Guidelines* (1988) to suggest administrative policies and program procedures for child welfare agencies serving the needs of children with HIV/AIDS.

There is still much more work to be done to ensure that all social service agencies embrace and institute appropriate policies and procedures to work with children and adolescents who are themselves HIV infected. At the same time, it is essential that attention be given to children who lose their parents to HIV/AIDS—children who may be HIV infected but who, in most instances, are not. CWLA and its National Task Force on Children and HIV Infection now focus their efforts on the burgeoning numbers of children who are "affected" by the HIV/AIDS epidemic as a result of their parents' deaths.

To address the needs of these children and their families effectively, it is important to recognize that all of these children, including those who are not HIV infected, have special needs. These youngsters may be older children, part of sibling groups, from minority or ethnic groups, affected by chronic illnesses, or affected by a range of health, mental health, and developmental disabilities. At the very least, they will be grieving the death of their parents. Their special needs, whether HIV-related or not, must be taken into account as their parents are helped to plan for them while still living. Whether the plan is legally recognized placement with kin or adoption by an unrelated family or by a family member, informal placement with kin, or guardianship, the child's full range of needs must be recognized and addressed in the recruitment and placement processes and in the provision of postplacement supports.

■ THE PURPOSE OF THESE GUIDELINES

These guidelines specifically address the issues of placing children who lose their parents to HIV/AIDS with kin and with adoptive families (who may be related to the child, unrelated to the child, or the child's foster family). A companion piece, *Because You Love Them: A Parent's Planning Guide,* accompanies these guidelines and helps parents who are HIV-infected to make plans for their children's future care. Parents can use this planning guide by themselves or with professionals in support groups and counseling sessions.

These guidelines are intended to help child welfare agencies develop culturally-competent, comprehensive kinship care and adoption services that respond to the needs of parents who are HIV infected, the needs of children who lose their parents to HIV/AIDS, and the needs of subsequent caregivers (adoptive and extended families) for these children. The guidelines are set out in six chapters: (1) Preparing for the Provision of Placement Services; (2) Outreach to and Support Services for Biological Parents and Other Caregivers Who Are HIV Positive; (3) Selecting Kin and Recruiting Adoptive Families; (4) Preparing Families and Children for Placement; (5) Postplacement Support Services; and (6) Advocacy and Collaboration. These chapters outline best practice and policy in working with this special population of children and their families, practice and policy that agencies can adapt to meet the specific needs of the families and children whom they serve. In addition, the appendixes contain a list of the CWLA subcommittee members who worked on these guidelines, a list of child welfare agencies working with HIV-affected families by state, a list of the Family Builders Network members, CWLA's position statement on mandatory testing, a description of the stages of HIV infection, a description of financial assistance programs, a description of tenets for support groups for individuals who are HIV infected and affected, a list of summer camps for children and families affected by HIV/AIDS, a suggested reading list, and a resource list of national organizations. Readers are urged to contact these organizations for regular updates, since this book can only reflect the state of knowledge as of 1995.

Definitions and Premises

These guidelines focus on two major types of permanency plans for children who lose their parents to HIV/AIDS: kinship care and adoption.

Kinship care is the full-time nurturing and protection of children by relatives, members of the tribe or clan, godparents, stepparents, or other adults who have a family bond with a child. "Parents and their relatives are free to arrange informal kinship care when issues relating to the safety and protection of children have not been brought to the attention of the child welfare system. Because parents have custody of the child, relatives need not be approved, licensed, or supervised by the state" [CWLA 1993].

When a child who must be separated from his/her parents can be placed safely with kin, they maintain their family connections, sense of belonging, history, continuity of culture, and often can live in the same community. Research has shown that kin are more likely to accept sibling groups, and the placements are more stable than those with non-relatives. For these reasons, CWLA recommends that kinship care be the first option assessed for children who must be separated from their parents.

CWLA [1988] defines adoption as "a child welfare service for children who cannot be cared for by their birth parents and who need and can benefit from the establishment of new and permanent family ties." The adoption material in this guide is based on two major premises. First, all children are adoptable. It cannot be assumed that any characteristic or combination of such characteristics as age, sibling group status, race or ethnicity, HIV status, and developmental difficulties make a child unadoptable. Aggressive recruitment of families often leads to the adoption of children with very special needs. Second, adoption is an emotional, social, and legal process for all members of the adoption triad (the biological family, adoptive family, and child).

According to CWLA [1988],

> Adopted individuals, biological families, and adoptive families are best served by a process that is open and honest; one that supports the concept that all information, including identifying information, may be shared between birth and adoptive parents. The concept of openness, while protecting the rights of the individuals involved, should be an integral part of all adoption services. The degree of openness in any adoption should be arrived at by mutual agreement based on a thoughtful, informed, decision-making process by the birth parents, the prospective adoptive parents, and the child, when appropriate.

Reflecting the philosophy of CWLA's earlier HIV guidelines, this document is also based on four premises regarding high quality service delivery for HIV-affected children and families:

- child welfare agencies must be equipped to provide specialized services for families who are HIV affected, including biological, extended, and adoptive families, in a culturally competent manner and with a high level of expertise and knowledge;

- child welfare personnel, caregivers, and communities must receive accurate educational information about HIV/AIDS in order to demystify the disease;

- service delivery to HIV-affected families must be child centered, family focused, and community based; and

- services must be coordinated across varying systems and agencies to meet the multifaceted needs of the child, the biological parents, adoptive parents, and the extended family.

■ SETTING THE STAGE: CHANGES IN THE HIV/AIDS PANDEMIC

When considering the growing phenomenon of children losing their parents to HIV/AIDS, it is important to recognize the impact of the AIDS epidemic on the larger society. In the United States, as of December 1993, a total of 361,164 persons were reported to have AIDS, and over one million persons were estimated to be HIV infected. At last report, AIDS was the leading cause of death for men aged 25-44, and for women, the fourth leading cause [CDC 1994].

Over time, the faces of persons with and affected by HIV/AIDS have dramatically changed. While the number of homosexual or bisexual men contracting AIDS has stabilized, the incidence of HIV disease among women is increasing. Data indicate that the fastest growing groups becoming infected with HIV are heterosexual women and adolescents, the vast majority of whom are African American and Latino.

Women and HIV/AIDS

Current statistics paint a troubling picture of the incidence of HIV among women. The CDC estimated in 1994 that between 55,000 and 75,000 women in the United States would have AIDS by 1995. In fact, it is predicted that since the infection rate in women has reached critical levels, by the year 2000, more than 50% of newly-infected adults worldwide will be women.

According to the American Association for World Health [1993], the percentage increase in new reported AIDS cases in 1992 in the United States was far greater among women (9%) than among men (2.5%). At the end of 1993, women made up over 13% of all AIDS cases in the U.S.—over 46,000 women had AIDS. Of these women, a disproportionate number are African American and Latina. Of women in the United States with AIDS, 54% are African American, 24% Caucasian, 21% Latina, 0.5% Asian/Pacific Islander, and 0.3% Native American [CDC 1994].

According to the CDC [1993], an estimated 7,000 women who are HIV infected give birth annually in the United States. Approximately 25% of infants born to women who are HIV infected will themselves contract the virus. There is a glimmer of hope that the transmission rate from mother to child will decrease as a result of a limited clinical trial (#076) administered by the National Institute of Allergies and Infectious Diseases (NIAID). Preliminary results show that AZT delivered to the mothers who participated in this clinical trial both antepartum (before the birth of their child) and intrapartum (during the birth of their child) and to the newborn during the first six weeks of life (beginning 8 to 12 hours after birth) significantly reduced the risk of perinatal transmission of HIV.

Because of the limited scope of the study, however, these results should not be over-generalized to represent all women living with HIV. Overall, the pregnant women who were HIV positive participating in this study should be considered as healthy, because a) they had not taken any antiretroviral therapy during their current pregnancy; b) they had basic CD4+ cell lymphocyte counts greater than 200; and c) they were in the earlier stages of HIV infection. While the results of this study are promising (the risk of perinatal transmission decreased from the national average of 25% to 8.3% when both the mother and child received AZT therapy), the NIAID has scheduled subsequent testing on the children born to mothers who participated in clinical trial #076 to determine the long-term consequences and benefits of AZT therapy.

Many trends in the HIV pandemic, whether it be the increase of HIV infection among women, the growing, disproportionate number of women of color among people with AIDS, or the potential downward turn of HIV perinatal transmission, will impact service delivery, prevention strategies, and policy development for women, children, and families. One other trend, the increase in infection through heterosexual contact, is equally significant. While approximately 49% of U.S. women became HIV positive through intravenous drug use, an increasing proportion of women (35%) are becoming infected through heterosexual contact.

Children and HIV/AIDS

As of December 1993, a reported 5,228 children in the United States were diagnosed as having AIDS, a 21% increase since 1992 and a 51% increase over 1991. Eighty-seven percent of these children were infected through perinatal transmission [CDC 1994]. Among children who contract HIV from their mothers, almost 14% will be diagnosed with AIDS in their first year, and 11-12% will be diagnosed in each of the following years through age 7—providing an estimated average age for definitive AIDS diagnosis of 4.1 years [MaWhimmey et al. 1993].

Because of medical advances and early identification, children infected with HIV in the 1990s have a much longer life expectancy than their counterparts in the 1980s. For approximately 80% of the children living with HIV, the virus has a latency period of six years. If the length of the latency period remains constant, many children who are HIV infected will outlive their parents, who are also HIV positive. Some children, however, will have short lives, depending on the stage of the mother's infection during pregnancy. Infants born to mothers with AIDS-defining illnesses (in women, typically pulmonary tuberculosis, recurrent pneumonia, and invasive cervical cancer) were three and a half times more likely to develop AIDS-related infections and four and a half times more likely to die within 18 months than children born to mothers who were HIV infected but presenting no AIDS-defining illnesses.

Characteristics of Children Who Will Lose Their Mothers to HIV/AIDS

As the number of women living with HIV escalates, the number of infected and affected children will continue to grow. Children who are infected are those who themselves are HIV positive. Children who are affected are those who are not necessarily HIV infected themselves but have a family member who is HIV positive. The impact of HIV/AIDS on children is not solely a national problem. While the numbers of U.S. children who will lose their parents to HIV/AIDS will reach critical levels by the year 2000, between 10 to 15 million children under the age of 10 living in sub-Saharan Africa will lose their parents to HIV/AIDS.

Two studies provide estimates on the numbers of children who will be affected in the United States. One by Michaels and Levine [1992] projects that by the year 2000 between 72,000 and 125,000 children and youths (and an additional 60,000 young adults over 18) will have lost their mothers to HIV/AIDS in the United States. Other data gathered by Caldwell, Fleming, and Oxtoby [1992] indicate that between 1992 and 2000, 93,000 to 112,000 uninfected children and 32,000 to 38,000 children who are infected with HIV will be born to mothers who are HIV infected. Michaels and Levine [1992] paint a portrait of children in the United States who will lose their parents to HIV/AIDS:

- the majority will not be HIV infected, but they will be at increased risk for developmental and behavioral problems;
- Eighty percent will be born to African American or Latina women;
- the majority will come from single-parent families and from poor communities; and
- approximately 50% will be adolescents between 13 and 18.

Of children who are projected to lose their parents to HIV/AIDS, 60% will be from six cities: New York City, Newark, Miami, San Juan, Los Angeles, and Washington, DC. The other 40% will be from other cities, suburbs, and rural areas [Levine and Stein 1994]. It is important to note that this problem will affect every urban and rural community—large or small—in varying magnitudes.

REFERENCES

American Association for World Health. (1993). *Time to act: Resource booklet*. Washington, DC: American Association for World Health.

Caldwell, M.B., Fleming, P., & Oxtoby, M. (1992). Estimated number of AIDS orphans in the United States. *Pediatrics, 90* (3), 482.

Centers for Disease Control and Prevention (CDC). (1994). *HIV/AIDS surveillance report, year-end edition*. Atlanta, GA: Author.

■ ■ ■

Centers for Disease Control and Prevention (CDC). (1993). *HIV/AIDS surveillance report, third quarter edition*. Atlanta, GA: Author.

Child Welfare League of America. (1988). *Report of the Task Force on Children and AIDS: Initial Guidelines*. Washington, DC: Author.

Child Welfare League of America. (1994). *Kinship Care: A Natural Bridge. The Report of the CWLA North American Kinship Care Policy and Practice Committee*. Washington, DC: Author.

Levine, C., & Stein, G. (1994). *Orphans of the HIV epidemic: Unmet needs in six U.S. cities*. New York: The Orphan Project.

MaWhimmey, F., Pagano, M., & Thomas, P. (1993, October). Age at AIDS diagnosis for children with perinatally acquired HIV. *Journal of Acquired Immune Deficiency Syndrome, 6* (10), 1139-1144.

Michaels, D., & Levine, C. (1992). Estimates of the number of motherless youth orphaned by AIDS in the United States. *Journal of the American Medical Association, 268,* 3456-3461.

National Institute of Allergies and Infectious Diseases (NIAID). (1994, February 21). AZT reduces rate of maternal transmission of HIV. Rockville, MD: Author.

Chapter 1

Preparing for the Provision of Placement Services

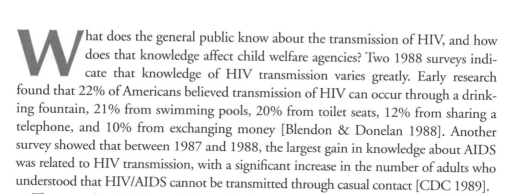

What does the general public know about the transmission of HIV, and how does that knowledge affect child welfare agencies? Two 1988 surveys indicate that knowledge of HIV transmission varies greatly. Early research found that 22% of Americans believed transmission of HIV can occur through a drinking fountain, 21% from swimming pools, 20% from toilet seats, 12% from sharing a telephone, and 10% from exchanging money [Blendon & Donelan 1988]. Another survey showed that between 1987 and 1988, the largest gain in knowledge about AIDS was related to HIV transmission, with a significant increase in the number of adults who understood that HIV/AIDS cannot be transmitted through casual contact [CDC 1989].

The general public's knowledge and feelings about HIV/AIDS seriously affect child welfare agencies. While current literature shows that the general public has become more knowledgeable about HIV/AIDS and its modes of transmission, significant numbers still fear its transmission. Misconceptions, coupled with inaccurate information and increasing numbers of affected children entering the schools, have contributed to hysteria about the disease and discrimination toward people with HIV/AIDS and those affected by it. The knowledge and feelings of the public as a whole will influence child welfare agencies in many respects: (a) the recruitment and retention of adoptive and foster parents who are willing to care for children who are HIV affected or infected; (b) the selection and preparation of kinship caregivers to take responsibility for the children; (c) the need for training and education for child welfare agency staff, foster and adoptive parents, kin, and direct service volunteers; and (d) the agency's HIV/AIDS prevention activities undertaken to educate young people and the community at large.

As the HIV epidemic broadens to affect heterosexual women and adolescents, child welfare agencies increasingly will be challenged to work with people with HIV/AIDS and/or their affected family members and friends. In the coming years, HIV/AIDS, in one form or another, will undoubtedly affect every agency and professional working in various child welfare settings.

Education and training of professionals who work with HIV-affected families is vital to helping them deliver services compassionately and effectively. Since the onset of the HIV/AIDS pandemic, a range of professionals, including social workers, nurses, and others, have been leaders in service provision and advocacy for individuals who are HIV infected and affected. Many professionals have struggled to continue working with families affected by HIV/AIDS, because the public's response to this health crisis has often been fear, hate, bigotry, and discrimination. Over time, professionals working with people with HIV/AIDS may experience despair, helplessness, hopelessness, stress, and isolation. Research shows that professionals working with people with HIV/AIDS benefit from education and training—it increases their knowledge about HIV/AIDS and enhances their ability to work effectively with their clients.

Education and training on HIV/AIDS issues are not only critical for professional child welfare staff, but also for adoptive and foster parents, kinship caregivers, and the children and youths served by child welfare agencies, as well as for all professionals working with families touched by HIV/AIDS. Each professional group, including child development specialists, social workers, nutritionists, juvenile justice workers, family court judges, mental health specialists, medical personnel, and educators, should have specific and complementary HIV/AIDS competencies and receive appropriate training. In addition, academic programs in these various disciplines should provide information on HIV/AIDS in the context of working with affected families.

When placing children who lose their parents to HIV/AIDS with other families, all members of the service paradigm (defined for these guidelines as professionals, biological parents, kin, adoptive parents, foster parents, and children) will need more than HIV/AIDS knowledge and expertise. Training and education must also focus on kinship- and adoption-related issues for this special population. Such issues as separation and loss, attachment and bonding, permanency planning, and the placement process must be covered.

This chapter focuses on three areas:

■ preparing all individuals within the service paradigm on HIV and adoption and kinship issues;

■ educating future professionals in degree programs, particularly social work, about HIV-related issues; and

- providing additional support services for professionals, students, and volunteers who work with persons infected with or affected by HIV/AIDS.

■ PREPARING PROFESSIONALS, BIOLOGICAL PARENTS, OTHER CAREGIVERS, AND CHILDREN ON HIV-RELATED ISSUES AND ADOPTION AND KINSHIP CARE

Child welfare professionals as a whole are not well prepared to deal with HIV-related issues and need special training and preparation to work effectively in this area. In one survey of 379 National Association of Social Work members about their knowledge of HIV/AIDS, Peterson [1991] found that 75% of the respondents did not believe they had a professional reason to learn about HIV/AIDS.

In addition to their lack of preparation and their perceptions that they do not need preparation in this area, many professionals do not have accurate knowledge about HIV/AIDS. According to Peterson [1991], more than 50% of the surveyed social workers answered the AIDS knowledge questions incorrectly, demonstrating an intensified need for AIDS education for social workers and other agency professionals. In a follow-up analysis to assess the differential knowledge social workers have of HIV/AIDS, Peterson [1992] found that only 28.1% of the AIDS-related questions about minority issues and 20.4% about gay issues were answered correctly.

Similarly, Gillman [1991, 598], in a survey of 357 practicing social workers affiliated with the Philadelphia Division of the National Association of Social Workers, found that while social workers have a keen interest in the issue of HIV/AIDS, they also "have many fears and misconceptions about AIDS that might impede empathic and competent service delivery to clients." Approximately 33% of the respondents said they were somewhat resistant to working with a client who was HIV infected. In addition, 20% of the respondents preferred not to have a person who was HIV positive within their caseloads because they did not know enough about AIDS and they did not want to work with terminally ill persons and intravenous drug users.

Zuger [1991] notes that physicians and other health care professionals are also reluctant to care for patients with HIV infection. Two surveys demonstrate this reluctance. In 1986, fewer than 50% of 325 American orthopedic surgeons agreed that they were ethically obligated to operate on HIV-infected patients in all situations in which surgery was medically indicated. Another 1986 survey showed that of 258 house officers at two large New York City residency programs, approximately 50% were mildly, moderately, or extremely resentful at having to take care of AIDS patients and 24% felt that refusing to care for AIDS patients was not unethical.

According to Zuger [1991], multiple factors contribute to this reluctance: 1) serving HIV-infected patients constitutes a risk to their health and their family's; 2) caring for HIV-infected individuals can be seen as a risk to practitioner's livelihood and as jeopardizing relationships with noninfected patients; 3) HIV-infected patients are considered difficult medically, potentially taxing the immediate competence of primary health caretakers and requiring subspeciality consultation, specialized treatments, and unfamiliar medications; 4) although AIDS patients can survive for years after diagnosis, their course is often seen as inexorably downhill; and 5) HIV-infected individuals are often considered undesirable simply by virtue of their risk groups.

When social workers and other professionals have the requisite knowledge, however, they are able to work effectively with people with HIV/AIDS. Gillman's research [1991] demonstrated that social workers with the most knowledge about HIV/AIDS had received training and were willing to provide services to people with HIV/AIDS. On the other hand, only 39% of the respondents had received inservice AIDS-related training, which was categorized as inadequate. In a survey of University of Kentucky social work alumni, Royse et al. [1987] found that greater knowledge of HIV/AIDS was associated with less fear and greater empathy for people with HIV/AIDS.

Similarly, in a study of hospital social workers, Wiener and Siegel [1990, 22] found that "social workers who had greater knowledge about the disease reported significantly higher levels of comfort in providing social work services to people with HIV/AIDS, reported significantly less fear of contracting AIDS through providing care to people with HIV/AIDS, and tended to be less homophobic than social workers who lacked such an understanding." This study also showed that of the social workers, 70.1% were highly comfortable working with terminally ill patients, 51.9% with children with AIDS, 48.1% with adults with AIDS, and 34.1% with drug abusers.

Social workers, like other professionals, know what information and training they need. The results of Gillman's research [1991], however, show there is often a discrepancy between the type of HIV/AIDS training social workers want and what they receive. For example, 90% of the social workers wanted training in clinical issues (psychosocial issues and individual and group support), but only 12% had received such training; 80% wanted additional knowledge about such community resources as case management, housing, hospicecare, counseling, and hotlines, but only 3% had received such information; 69% wanted medical and preventive information on HIV, including symptoms, treatment, research, and transmission, but only 20% had received such information; and 76% of the social workers wanted training in death and dying issues, but only 2% had received such training.

Child welfare agencies must be prepared to train all members of the service paradigm with up-to-date information on HIV infection and AIDS. Education and training components should include:

1. demographics of the HIV/AIDS pandemic;
2. basic medical information and disease characteristics;
3. transmission of HIV and other infectious diseases, including prevention, and infection control and universal precaution procedures;
4. caring for people with HIV/AIDS;
5. HIV testing;

6. confidentiality and disclosure; and

7. cultural competence and HIV/AIDS.

In addition to HIV/AIDS-related information, all members of the service paradigm need to receive education and training on permanency planning alternatives, including adoption and kinship care. Training components might include:

8. permanency planning for children who lose their parents to AIDS;

9. psychosocial issues for biological, adoptive, and extended families;

10. support and core services for biological, adoptive, and extended families;

11. financial assistance programs for adoptive and kinship families;

12. coordination of service delivery and advocacy; and

13. grief and bereavement.

The sample training and course outline (Table 1) details specific content for each of these 13 training components. The suggested education and training outline should be tailored to meet the needs of the target audiences: professionals, biological parents, kinship caregivers, adoptive parents, and children and youths. In the case of professionals and adoptive parents, these training components should supplement the training that the agency provides. In the case of kin, child welfare agencies should supplement their orientation/preparation program. Child welfare agencies should determine the goals and objectives for training each target audience, and plan ongoing educational activities accordingly. They should ascertain for each target audience the level of detail and depth of information needed in each of the 13 core training components.

Training should reflect the agency's philosophy of serving families who are HIV affected and the goal of creating new families through adoption and kinship care for those children who need this service. It should focus equally on HIV-related material, on the one hand, and on securing adoptive and extended families for children with special needs or parenting these children, depending on the audience. The training must be culturally competent and age- and development-appropriate. Education and training activities should encourage a cooperative, respectful, and team-building relationship and a dynamic partnership between families and staff members. It should be delivered by an interdisciplinary faculty, drawing from local experts in the fields of child welfare, health care, pastoral care, mental health, and family court law. All training materials should be user friendly, with trainers using appropriate terminology and handouts and adapting their presentation for the specific audience.

Issues Specific to the Education of Children and Youths

Over 50% of the children and youths who will lose their parents to HIV/AIDS by the year 2000 will be between the ages of 13 and 18. An additional 60,000 young adults over the age of 18 will also lose their parents to this disease. Prospective adoptive parents and kin who may provide ongoing care for these young people will need to know

TABLE 1
Sample Education and Training Course Outline

(Adapt for social workers, biological parents, adoptive and kinship families, children, and youths)

I. DEMOGRAPHICS OF THE HIV/AIDS PANDEMIC
- A. HIV/AIDS as a disease affecting families
- B. HIV/AIDS as a disease affecting the child welfare system

II. BASIC MEDICAL INFORMATION
- A. Definition of infectious disease
- B. Definition of HIV
- C. Definition of AIDS
- D. Progression (continuum of events) of HIV to AIDS
  - 1. In men
  - 2. In women
  - 3. In children

III. TRANSMISSION OF HIV AND OTHER INFECTIOUS DISEASES
- A. Modes of transmission
  - 1. Sexual intercourse
    - a. vaginal
    - b. oral
    - c. anal
  - 2. Blood-to-blood
    - a. injection drug use
    - b. professional exposure
  - 3. Mother to child
    - a. perinatal
    - b. breast milk
- B. Myths about the transmission of HIV
  - 1. Kissing
  - 2. Touching
  - 3. Playing
  - 4. Mosquitos and monkeys
  - 5. Toilets
  - 6. Other

- C. Preventing the transmission of all infectious diseases
  - 1. Infection control procedures
  - 2. Universal precautions procedures
  - 3. T.B.
- D. Preventing HIV transmission
  - 1. Sexual abstinence
  - 2. Safer sex
  - 3. Nonsharing of needles
  - 4. Other precautions
  - 5. Clinical Trial 076

IV. CARING FOR PEOPLE WITH HIV/AIDS
- A. Symptoms of adults with HIV/AIDS
  - 1. In men
  - 2. In women
- B. Caring for adults with HIV/AIDS
- C. Symptoms of children with HIV/AIDS
- D. Caring for children with HIV/AIDS

V. HIV TESTING
- A. Meaning of the HIV antibody test
  - 1. The Western Blot/ELISA
  - 2. HIV Culture or PCR test
  - 3. p24 Antigen test
- B. When testing is appropriate for children and adults
- C. Pre- and post-test counseling
- D. Confidentiality and disclosure of HIV testing information

VI. CONFIDENTIALITY AND DISCLOSURE
- A. Need to know
- B. Duty to warn

VII. CULTURAL COMPETENCE AND AIDS

A. How different cultures respond to AIDS in different and similar ways

B. Appropriate interventions for different cultures

C. Respecting cultural differences and similarities

D. Religious beliefs

VIII. PERMANENCY PLANNING FOR CHILDREN WHO LOSE THEIR PARENTS TO HIV/AIDS

A. Assisting parents with making legal, permanent care arrangements for children

B. Permanency planning options
1. Kinship care
2. Adoption (unrelated, relative, and foster parent)
3. Standby guardianship
4. Guardianship
5. Voluntary placement of children in out-of-home foster care

C. Financial assistance programs for new caregivers

IX. PSYCHOSOCIAL ISSUES FOR BIOLOGICAL, ADOPTIVE, AND EXTENDED FAMILIES

A. Feelings of people with HIV/AIDS and their affected family members
1. Parents who are HIV infected
   a. denial
   b. shame
   c. anger
   d. devastation
   e. depression
   f. guilt
   g. isolation and fear
2. Children who are HIV infected or affected
   a. grief and loss
   b. confusion
   c. anger and resentment
   d. sibling rivalry
   e. shame
   f. school issues
   g. denial
   h. depression

B. Helping parents to tell children about a diagnosis of HIV
1. If, when, and how to tell children who themselves are HIV infected
2. If, when, and how to tell children about parents' HIV infection
3. Children's reactions
4. Coping mechanisms

C. Working with adoptive and kinship families on special issues
1. Separation and loss
   a. relationship between biological parents, extended family members, and prospective adoptive parents
   b. sibling relationships
2. Attachment and bonding
   a. relationship between biological family, extended family, and prospective adoptive parents and children
   b. co-parenting
3. Other psychological and clinical issues
   a. suicidal ideation
   b. mediation skills

X. SUPPORT AND CORE SERVICES FOR BIOLOGICAL, ADOPTIVE AND EXTENDED FAMILIES

A. Counseling

B. Drug treatment

C. Food assistance

D. Homemakers

E. Hospice care

F. Information (hotlines and clearinghouses)

G. Medical care
1. Clinical trials
2. Treatment alternatives

H. Recreational services

I. Respite care

J. School services for children with special needs

K. Support groups
1. For biological parents
2. For kin
3. For adoptive parents
4. For children and youths
5. For staff

L. Transportation

XI. FINANCIAL ASSISTANCE PROGRAMS FOR ADOPTIVE AND KINSHIP FAMILIES

A. AFDC

B. Federal Adoption Assistance and State Adoption Subsidies

C. Foster Care Maintenance Rates (Title IV-E)

D. Guardianship subsidies

E. Housing programs

F. Medicaid

G. Nutrition programs
1. Food Stamps
2. WIC

H. Ryan White Care Act

I. Social Security Payments
1. Social Security Disability
2. Supplemental Security Income
3. Social Security Survivors Benefits

XII. COORDINATION OF SERVICE DELIVERY AND ADVOCACY

A. Case management and service coordination

B. Access to support and core services and financial assistance programs

C. Understanding applicable laws and regulations

D. Discrimination against people with HIV/AIDS

E. Complexity of families

XIII. GRIEF AND BEREAVEMENT

A. Death and dying
1. Losing someone you love
2. Recognizing grief and bereavement in self and others
3. Coping mechanisms

B. Methods for helping grieving children
1. At home
2. In a therapeutic setting

that while only a small percentage of these youths will already be HIV infected at the time of their parent's death, many others may be at increased risk of HIV infection. Because they may be experiencing overwhelming feelings of grief, loss, pain, and guilt, which increase their emotional vulnerability, they are more likely to engage in risk behaviors. All child welfare agencies, therefore, should provide HIV prevention education to all young people, extended family members, and adoptive parents. Prospective caregivers should be asked to help facilitate children's opportunities to participate in educational activities focused on prevention.

Kin, adoptive parents, and other caregivers need to support developmentally-appropriate education for children and youths about sexuality, sexual activity, sexual orientation, and the use of alcohol and other drugs, especially injection drugs, including any mind-altering substances. This education, while encouraging healthy feelings of self-esteem and sexuality, should provide young people with the necessary information to prevent the transmission of HIV or other sexually transmitted diseases (STDs). A two-pronged prevention approach is needed, with messages that encourage both sexual abstinence and, if young people are sexually active, correct and consistent use of barrier protections, such as disposable latex gloves and latex condoms, including application, removal, and disposal. This instruction should be given by individuals who are knowledgeable, sensitive, and comfortable with the material.

As with adults, children and youths need more than just the facts regarding HIV transmission and treatment. Research shows that although many young people understand how HIV is transmitted, they do not change their risky behaviors. Creative activities, including the use of peer education, role plays, experiential exercises, and the arts (drawing and drama), can help young people change their behaviors. Child welfare agencies working with runaway and homeless youths should consider showing prevention videos that use teen actors. In addition, organizations should consider utilizing trainings from local HIV and youth-serving agencies. Prevention education may be offered in support group sessions for children and young people who are losing or have lost their parents to HIV/AIDS. Emphasis should be placed on managing peer pressure; healthy decision making; coping with grief and bereavement; managing separation, loss, and anger; and building self-esteem.

The National Community AIDS Partnership [1993] outlines the following eight principles of successful HIV interventions for youth:

1. young people should be involved in every aspect of the program, including design, implementation, and evaluation;

2. programs should be developmentally appropriate;

3. programs must be accurate, honest, and frank;

4. young people need to learn and practice a repertoire of HIV risk-reduction skills;

5. young people need both physical and social resources and supports to maintain healthy behavior;

6. society needs to encourage and support healthy behavior;

7. adolescents with special needs (developmental delays and mental health problems) must be given special attention; and

8. evaluations must be structured around measurable goals. These principles can be applied to various methods of peer education, support groups, and experiential exercises as well as arts activities.

A few peer education efforts have received national recognition. Intimate Realities, a dance troupe of 12 African American, Latino, and Caucasian teenagers in Yonkers, New York, and Teen TAPP (Teen Teatro AIDS Prevention Project), a group of five Latino peer educators in San Antonio, Texas, give performances to schools and community groups. Teen TAPP peer educators also receive training in cultural and sexual sensitivity and drama, and they use stories from their own lives to develop their performances.

■ EDUCATING FUTURE PROFESSIONALS IN DEGREE PROGRAMS ABOUT HIV-RELATED ISSUES

Both graduate and undergraduate students, especially those in social work, law, and health-related fields, need to understand the HIV pandemic and how it affects society, individuals, and families. Yet research indicates that social work students and those studying health disciplines are not being prepared to work with people with HIV/AIDS, their affected family members, and their friends. Frequently, students in social work and other related disciplines graduate without receiving any information on or experience in working with HIV/AIDS and related issues.

Two surveys underscore this concern. In a survey of 61 second-year graduate social work students at the University of California-Berkeley, Wexler [1989] found that students had limited knowledge about minorities, alcohol and other drug use, and diagnostic issues related to HIV/AIDS. Fewer than 20% of these students felt adequately prepared to provide services or advocate for people with AIDS and HIV-affected family members and communities. Harrison, Zurschmiede, and Sowers-Hoag's 1990 survey of both graduate and undergraduate social work students revealed that students felt professionally unprepared to work on HIV/AIDS-related issues.

As with professionals and adoptive and extended families, HIV/AIDS education for students should help them to identify their attitudes about HIV/AIDS, develop skills to work with those who are HIV positive and their affected family members, and learn concepts of death, dying, separation, and loss unique to HIV infection/AIDS.

Furthermore, students need to acquire knowledge about HIV/AIDS, including information on transmission, symptoms, treatment (experimental drugs and clinical trials), testing, confidentiality, prevention, infection control, and universal precautions. It is the responsibility of educators in various disciplines to incorporate this knowledge into their curricula. Child welfare agency field placements can provide students with HIV education through inservice training. In addition, child welfare professionals who work with people with HIV/AIDS should teach the needed knowledge and skills as adjunct professors in various disciplines. Whichever educational strategies are employed, they should be culturally sensitive and audience specific.

One strategy to help prepare future professionals is for academic disciplines to increase the number of field placements or internships that expose students to persons who are HIV infected and affected. These placements and internships could be in such locations as hospitals, child welfare agencies, public health departments, and community-based AIDS organizations. Students who work with people with HIV/AIDS in their field placements will need supportive resources to serve this population. In a survey of social work students working with people with HIV/AIDS, Silberman [1991] found these resources to be the most helpful (in descending order):

- informal discussions with other professionals in field placement sites;
- staff support groups in field placement agencies;

■ discussions with field supervisors and informal discussions with faculty/peers at school; and

■ class discussions.

Field placement students or interns, like professionals, need to be educated about HIV/AIDS before they work with this population, and need continuing education opportunities during their field placement or internship.

Other strategies to prepare future professionals include the use of role plays and inviting guest lecturers into the classroom. Role plays and guest speakers can help students learn the following:

■ empathy for individuals with HIV disease;

■ anxiety reduction techniques in working with people before and after their diagnosis;

■ coping strategies for grief and anticipatory mourning for people who are HIV infected and their affected family members and friends;

■ strategies to develop a comfort level and skills to discuss issues related to sex, alcohol and other drug use, and death and dying with their clients; and

■ empowerment techniques that help their clients to engage in risk-free behaviors.

Guest speakers may include those who have been affected by this epidemic, including people with HIV/AIDS, health care professionals, affected family members, lawyers, and social workers. In addition to social work, other academic disciplines, such as medicine, law, education, and counseling, should invite child welfare agency personnel who have expertise in HIV/AIDS and its impact on children, families, and society to serve as guest speakers.

Miller and Dane [1990, 185] sum up the need for HIV education for students: "Because practice with people with HIV/AIDS requires consideration of numerous issues, including, but not limited to, confidentiality, poverty, women's rights, human sexuality and sexual expression, the meaning of family, social work and health care, death, dying and bereavement, issues of minorities and other disfranchised groups, stigma, discrimination, and human rights, it seems untenable that any student should complete his or her (social work) education without AIDS as a fundamental reference point."

Educators must also receive HIV/AIDS training to help them understand the many dimensions of this disease. Educators, like agency professionals, field instructors, and students, can benefit from training that gives them the opportunity to discover their own feelings about HIV; determine their values and attitudes about heterosexuality, homosexuality, injection drug use, and death and dying; and reflect on their own experiences with HIV/AIDS. Colleges and universities should make their training available to local agencies as a community HIV/AIDS education resource. Advanced training for educators is needed to help them incorporate AIDS material into various curricula and create field placement and volunteer opportunities for students to work on HIV-related issues.

■ ■ ■ ■ ■

■ SUPPORTING PROFESSIONALS, STUDENTS, AND VOLUNTEERS WHO WORK WITH PERSONS INFECTED WITH AND AFFECTED BY HIV/AIDS

HIV/AIDS-related work can be emotionally draining. Professionals need to be reenergized and have their resources augmented to meet the increasing demands of working with this vulnerable population. In addition to inservice training, described earlier, professionals, volunteers, and students who work with persons infected with and affected by HIV need additional supports.

It is understandable that professionals who have done HIV/AIDS work for an extended period of time can become discouraged, disheartened, and burned out by the newest challenges of the HIV epidemic—children who lose their parents to HIV/AIDS and the growing ranks of women and young children who are HIV infected. At a time when there is no end in sight to this public health crisis, supports for professionals are most vital. Supports can reduce staff turnover, increase the cohesion of a program, boost coping capacities, and help maintain the quality of services for clients.

Agencies can provide an array of supports to help professionals continue doing AIDS work. These include: (a) establishing support groups; (b) providing flex-time and additional vacation time; (c) establishing realistic workloads; (d) providing training opportunities (conferences and workshops); and (e) increasing professional salary levels.

Support Groups

Support groups are one way to help professionals working with people with HIV/AIDS to garner the emotional strength—through shared experiences—to continue their work. Professionals may harbor anger toward colleagues who are unwilling to work with people with HIV/AIDS, at people with AIDS themselves, and at their own families, who may not support their work. They also may simply be exhausted by the demands of their work. Effective support groups may help staff in many ways. They may be able to find renewed meaning in their work; provide mutual support; reduce and manage stress; prevent burnout; cope with death and dying; work through their feelings, including depression and anger; and celebrate the lives of clients who have touched their lives.

Grossman and Silverstein [1993] have outlined ways to increase the effectiveness of support groups for those who work with people with HIV/AIDS and their affected family members and friends. Individual groups should be created for different professions, such as social workers and nurses. Participation should be voluntary, and those who attend should be encouraged to share their feelings. Groups should have 15 or fewer persons. And the facilitator must have experience with people with HIV/AIDS and be knowledgeable about group processes, including ways to positively direct communication. A suggested format for support group sessions is to organize panels of individuals who can highlight the rewarding aspects of HIV/AIDS work, including the opportunities for spiritual growth.

Flexible Work Schedules and Activities

Flexible work schedules are being used in child welfare agencies as a staff retention mechanism [Helfgott 1991]. Options include permanent part-time status, a compressed work week, job sharing, and reduced work time (a temporary part-time schedule that can be adjusted to full time when circumstances change). Child welfare agencies should consider providing professionals who work with HIV-affected families the benefit of flexible work schedules. Since the progression of HIV disease can be unpredictable, professionals may be required to work nontraditional hours, and a flex-time policy can support their work. In addition, by establishing procedures by which professionals doing HIV/AIDS work are rotated in and out of various services, agencies can help prevent burnout.

Realistic Workloads

Realistic workloads are necessary for child welfare personnel to provide effective services to their clients. While small workloads do not guarantee a high level of performance, heavy workloads do impair the quality of services [Hess 1991; Katz 1990; Shulman 1977]. Manageable workloads can be linked to staff retention. One survey, for example, found that former employees cited unrealistic workloads as their prime reason for leaving jobs. Professionals working with people with HIV/AIDS and their affected family members, like others working with people with terminal illnesses, especially need realistic workloads because of the severity of cases and the intensity of services provided.

No national workload standard exists for professionals who work with people with HIV/AIDS. Table 2 details some important factors child welfare agencies should take into account in determining the appropriate caseload for professionals working with this population.

Training Opportunities

All professionals need the opportunity to develop and enhance their skills and knowledge base. This is especially true for professionals who work with people with HIV/AIDS and their affected family members. Because information about HIV/AIDS accumulates and changes so rapidly, these professionals must have the opportunity to keep current with treatment modalities, clinical interventions, medical advances and clinical trials, life expectancy, legal principles, and national and community resources. Child welfare agencies should provide their employees with the opportunity to participate in conferences and training.

Salaries

Salaries should reflect professionals' education and experience, the level and intensity of services they provide, and the demands that their work places on them. They should be based on salary standard levels set by CWLA and NASW (National Association of Social Workers). Failure to adequately compensate professionals who work in intense and demanding settings, such as work with people with HIV/AIDS, can be demoraliz-

TABLE 2
Factors in Determining Workload

ADMINISTRATIVE ISSUES
- required attendance at staff meetings
- level of administrative functions
- need for evening work and weekend on-call status
- amount of supervision, consultation, and collaboration needed/provided
- attendance at staff development activities
- amount of time needed for reading job-related materials

SERVICE PROVISION
- size of the geographical area served
- size and composition of families served
- case complexity and severity
- estimated duration and intensity of needed services, treatment and outreach activities
- crisis orientation of the work
- frequency of caseload emergencies
- frequency of telephone contacts
- worker skill and experience
- availability of HIV/AIDS services in the geographic area

OTHER
- court schedules
- effectiveness of interagency relationships and processes
- community attitudes
- availability of legal counsel
- projected changes in caseloads

Adapted from Helfgott, 1991, Gardner 1985, and CWLA, 1988.

ing and, ultimately, contribute to high turnover. Social workers as a whole have traditionally been poorly paid, a factor in burnout. Child welfare agencies need to ensure that professionals who work with people with HIV/AIDS or in other commensurate positions are appropriately compensated in salary, benefits, and support.

REFERENCES

Blendon, R.J., & Donelan, K. (1988). Discrimination against people with AIDS: The public's perspective. *New England Journal of Medicine, 319,* 1022-1026.

Centers for Disease Control (CDC). (1989, May). HIV Epidemic and AIDS: Trends in knowledge—United States, 1987 and 1988. *Morbidity and Mortality Weekly Report, 38* (20), 353-358.

Garner, E. (1985). Information please. *Child Welfare LXIV* (2), 173-175.

Gillman, R. (1991). From resistance to rewards: Social workers' experiences and attitudes toward AIDS. *Families in Society: The Journal of Contemporary Human Services, 72* (10), 593-601.

Grossman, A. H., & Silverstein, C. (1993). Facilitating support groups for professionals working with people with AIDS. *Social Work,* 38(2), 144-151.

Harrison, D.F,. Zurschmiede, D.D., & Sowers-Hoag, K. (1990, March). *AIDS: Are students prepared for the continuing crisis in the 1990s?* Paper presented at the Council on Social Work Education Annual Program Meeting, Reno, NV.

Helfgott, K. (1991). *Staffing the child welfare agency: Recruitment and retention.* Washington, DC: Child Welfare League of America.

Hess, P. (1991). The impact of caseload size and caseworker/supervisor turnover on foster care reentry. First interim report of the professional review action project. Indianapolis, IN: Unpublished.

Katz, L. (1990). Effective permanency planning for children in foster care. *Social Work, 35* (3), 220-226.

Miller, S.O., & Dane, B.O. (1990). AIDS and social work: Curricula development in an epidemic. *Journal of Social Work Education, 2,* 177-186.

National Community AIDS Partnership. (1993). HIV prevention and youth: A guide for program development. Washington, DC: Author.

Peterson, K.J. (1991). Social workers knowledge about AIDS: A national survey. *Social Work, 36,* 31-37.

Peterson, K.J. (1992). Social workers' knowledge about AIDS: Working with vulnerable and oppressed people. *Health and Social Work, 17* (2), 116-127.

Royse, D., Dhooper, S., & Hatch, L. (1987). Undergraduate and graduate students' attitudes toward AIDS. *Psychological Reports, 60* (3), 1185-1186.

Shulman, L. (1977). *The impact of reduced caseloads on preventative services.* Vancouver, BC: University of British Columbia, School of Social Work.

Silberman, J.M. (1991). The AIDS epidemic: Professional and personal concerns of graduate social work students in field placement. *Social Work in Health Care, 15* (3), 77-100.

Wexler, S. (1989). Social welfare students and AIDS: A survey of knowledge, attitudes and professional preparation. *Journal of Teaching in Social Work, 3,* 131-149.

Wiener, L.S., & Siegel, K. (1990). Social workers' comfort in providing services to AIDS patients. *Social Work, 35,* 18-25.

Zuger, A. (1991). AIDS and the obligations of health care professionals. In F. Reamer, *AIDS and Ethics.* New York: Columbia University Press.

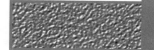

Chapter 2

Outreach to and Support Services for Biological Parents and Other Caregivers Who Are HIV Positive

The estimated number of children who will soon lose their parents to HIV/AIDS is staggering—72,000-125,000 by the year 2000—and growing numbers of families are in immediate need of assistance. However, HIV-affected individuals and families do not readily seek out services and support. Both public and voluntary child welfare agencies who serve families and who have programs designed to place children who lose their parents to HIV/AIDS with adoptive and extended families report low participation of parents who are HIV positive. These agencies include those located in HIV epicenters, like New York, Newark, Miami, Los Angeles, Chicago, and Washington, DC. Other child welfare agencies that anticipate serving HIV-affected families as part of their work report that not one family has come to their agency.

In response to the rising number of children who lose their parents to HIV/AIDS, CWLA completed a survey of 200 of its member agencies in March 1995 to determine agency programs and practices regarding placing children affected by HIV/AIDS with adoptive and extended families. Sixty-six (33%) of the child welfare agencies returned the survey, with 15 of these agencies indicating that they do not know if they serve families affected by HIV.

Some agencies do not keep records of children who are HIV affected. The 51 agencies that do keep statistics on HIV-affected families reported that of the 8,814 children with special needs they placed in permanent care arrangements in 1994, 548, or 6.2%, were HIV affected. Given the burgeoning number of families affected by HIV/AIDS, these figures demonstrate both that many families are not seeking support and that many agencies are unable to track HIV status as a special need. This survey identified a number of agencies with innovative programs serving HIV-affected families. They are listed in Appendix B by state.

The survey shows that it is critical that child welfare agencies proactively reach out to biological parents or other caregivers who are HIV positive, including those who are illegal immigrants predominantly living in HIV epicenters, and encourage them to participate in programs to help plan for their children's future care. It is also critical that these program titles should be positive and supportive (such as "My Sister's Children" in Virginia Beach, Virginia) to create an environment within which the families can feel included rather than identified and isolated. During outreach, child welfare agencies must also be prepared to meet biological parents' other needs, such as housing, homemaker services, support groups, and medical care. Typically, many of these service needs will have to be addressed before a family can begin making plans for their children's future care.

■ OUTREACH

Child welfare agencies must use vigorous strategies to locate parents who are HIV positive and involve them in their programs to place their children with kin and adoptive families. Outreach to identify and connect with biological parents should combine:

- word of mouth;
- public education campaigns; and
- locating child welfare satellite offices in public health clinics, housing projects, hospitals, places of worship, community-based AIDS service organizations, neighborhood organizations and gathering places, and other highly visible places.

Word of Mouth

Parents living with HIV/AIDS who participate in an established program to help them plan for themselves and their children's future are perhaps the best means of reaching other biological families. People living with HIV/AIDS gather at support groups, places of worship, health clinics, and funerals. Parents who are pleased with the services they are receiving are likely to spread the word about such a program and the available services, locations, hours of operation, fees, and staff, especially if they are asked to do so or are hired as outreach workers. In developing programs, agencies should consider training a parent living with HIV/AIDS to provide community outreach services. In addition, after such events as support groups and funerals where people with HIV/AIDS meet, child welfare agencies should expect and plan for an increase in program referrals. Agencies will find that the word-of-mouth principle also applies in recruiting adoptive families and identifying kin.

Public Education Campaigns

Child welfare agencies should develop state and local collaborations to produce multi-level, culturally competent public education campaigns to reach biological parents, kin, adoptive parents, or other prospective caregivers. Effective campaigns will create linkages with culturally competent community-based organizations, and include the development of (a) print materials such as brochures, posters, print ads, billboards, and organizational newsletters; (b) broadcast materials such as television and radio spots; and (c) special outreach activities. All campaign components should target the neighborhoods and communities most greatly affected by the HIV/AIDS epidemic. Agencies serving communities with growing numbers of Latinos, Haitians, and Asian/Pacific Islanders who are HIV positive should also produce materials in Spanish, Creole, and other languages, as appropriate. These materials must respect the fact that most women who are HIV infected do not want to be singled out and identified as such.

Different public education products require distinct levels of effort and expertise to develop. Child welfare agency public relations departments should play integral roles in developing and implementing public education strategies. While it is more costly than going it alone, some agencies may find it necessary and helpful to engage a public relations consulting firm to develop a media plan. Others may find it useful to seek assistance from the local advertising council, which will have expertise in media productions and may donate time to the community. One step in developing a plan is to organize focus groups of no more than 10 parents and their affected family members to find out their thoughts, ideas, and feelings about planning for their children's future, as well as their suggestions for appropriate public education messages. Another approach is to have staff survey clients about their needs. Suggestions on how to proceed in developing these various media components are given below.

Print Media

Print materials are an important vehicle for reaching out to parents, for they can be targeted to specific communities without incurring great costs. Child welfare agencies must decide on the target audiences for their brochures, posters, print ads, and billboards. The messages and slogans should be brief, clearly written, easily understandable, and free of jargon. They must not exploit the HIV-infected or -affected families, avoiding "AIDS orphans" or other emotionally charged terms. In brochures targeted to biological parents who are HIV positive, any reference to HIV/AIDS should be removed from the cover, because those who have not yet told their families of their illness will hesitate to pick up a brochure that has *HIV* or *AIDS* splashed across the front.

In all print materials, design is important to ensuring use. Effective use of bright colors and striking layouts, including culturally inclusive pictures and ample white space, are critical. In some cases, graphics, because of their universal appeal, suit multicultural populations better than photos of individuals. If possible, the message, slogan, design, and colors used for various print materials should be coordinated. The people pictured in print materials should reflect the racial, ethnic, gender, cultural, and religious diversity of the agency's clientele and should not perpetuate stereotypes. Program brochures and posters should be distributed to public health clinics, hospitals, places of worship, and AIDS service organizations.

While typically expensive, billboards present another good opportunity for public education, and should be considered in neighborhoods with a high incidence of HIV infection and AIDS. Agencies might also consider public service space in public transportation systems.

Print ads, news and feature articles, and letters to the editor in response to HIV/AIDS issues are other forms of media that child welfare agencies can employ in outreach to families. Agencies should target not only their large local newspapers, but also community papers, which may be more likely to run feature stories and stories of community interest. Agencies may also want to target alternative newspapers in the gay and lesbian community.

Broadcast Media

Opportunities for educating the public through the broadcast media include radio and television public service announcements, talk shows, news shows, and public affairs programs. Child welfare agencies can develop either 30- or 60-second public service announcements (PSAs) that give information about issues or specific activities related to their programs. In developing PSAs, agency professionals should write a clear, crisp, and brief script, free of emotionally charged terms, that repeats the slogans and messages used in print materials. Radio stations typically prefer that their own announcers read the PSAs. Staff and board members should deliver the PSAs in person by appointment to the public service directors at the stations. Child welfare agency public relations professionals should follow up with the public service directors, urging them to use the announcements during peak listening hours as well as at other times. Agency personnel should send thank-you letters to the radio stations that use the PSAs. In large cities, agencies may find it helpful to send PSAs to radio stations that target certain ethnic and cultural groups.

Child welfare agencies might also explore local television and radio programs to announce their services, and in turn, recruit biological parents, kinship caregivers, and adoptive parents. The public relations department or individual who coordinates communication activities should target local reporters who have an interest in adoption or AIDS-related issues. In designing broadcast strategies, agencies should focus on the following: local radio talk shows that commonly present human interest stories, local television news shows that feature families and children or innovative local happenings, public affairs programming on television, and cable programming. Child welfare agencies should recognize the potential of the media to sensationalize stories, and should work with reporters and others to present clear and accurate pictures that avoid judgment of parents who are HIV positive.

Television and radio reporters are likely to want to interview biological and adoptive parents. Child welfare professionals should decide which parents may be most comfortable in being interviewed and then approach them to see if they are willing. If parents agree to be interviewed, it will be important for agency public relations professionals or others who are knowledgeable about public relations to prepare media personnel and parents. This may include holding practice question and answer sessions and discussing ways to maintain composure and control during interviews. Coaching and preparation are central to good interviews, and cannot be overlooked. Child welfare agencies also need to counsel parents about the feedback they may receive from relatives, friends, and strangers, and advise them about their right to maintain their confidentiality, insisting the media alter voices and shoot "back shots." Agency professionals should accompany the parents to the sessions with reporters.

Special Outreach Activities

One special media activity is the use of video for recruitment purposes. In developing videos to inform and recruit biological parents who are HIV positive, child welfare agencies should work closely with biological parents, kin, adoptive parents, and children presently receiving services to make their stories part of the video presentation. The video content might include biological parents encouraging others in similar circumstances to consider planning for their children, tips on how they can build relationships with extended family and prospective adoptive parents, suggestions on ways to enhance their relationships with their children, and discussions on how to work closely with professionals to develop and ensure the implementation of plans. This strategy can also be used to identify kin and recruit adoptive parents.

As with broadcast media, child welfare agencies will need to prepare parents and children for videotaping. In addition, child welfare agencies should, if possible, enlist the support of a local or national celebrity or media personality to narrate the video. The development of professionally completed videos is normally very expensive. Consequently child welfare agencies may have to enhance existing collaborative partnerships with television and radio stations, video companies, corporations, and foundations, develop new partnerships, or form a statewide coalition of similar agencies to undertake such a venture.

Other means that agencies may use to spread the message include slide shows, speakers' bureaus, theater productions, and community-based activities, such as those connected to places of worship, schools, and day care centers.

Locating Child Welfare Satellite Offices

Some child welfare agencies have located satellite offices in public health clinics, housing projects, hospitals, places of worship, community-based AIDS service organizations, and other visible places where people with HIV/AIDS congregate. Satellite offices in such locations increase the visibility of child welfare agencies to vulnerable populations. Agencies will need to make a special effort to reach out to illegal immigrants, finding places where they feel comfortable and are not afraid to seek services. Agencies that do not undertake this satellite strategy should develop collaborations with other agencies serving people with HIV/AIDS. At the very least, child welfare agencies should supply their print materials to these other agencies for distribution to clients.

■ SUPPORT SERVICES

Child welfare agencies that employ rigorous outreach strategies to recruit biological families into their programs must also be prepared to provide or link them with services that meet their emerging needs. Throughout their illness, biological parents will need an array of services to help them manage their lives and to plan for their children's future. Some of these services are described in the following pages.

Housing
People with HIV/AIDS and their family members need adequate housing. Housing programs that serve not only the individual with HIV/AIDS but also the entire family unit affected by the disease are particularly valuable. Child welfare agencies placing children affected by HIV/AIDS will find that they will be increasingly confronted by families' housing needs, including means of accessing rent and utility subsidies.

Homemaker Services
Homemaker services can help biological parents living with HIV/AIDS maintain themselves in their home longer than would otherwise be possible. In some states, homemaker services are only available for the person who is HIV infected, and do not cover children in the home. In these states, child welfare agencies need to advocate for changes in state policies.

Support Groups
Support groups are an important way for biological parents living with HIV/AIDS to share feelings and receive and give support. Support group members frequently raise questions about HIV and its transmission modes, medical advances, current treatments and protocols, services, and financial assistance available to people with AIDS and their families. These groups can help parents overcome their feelings of guilt and denial and encourage them to begin planning for their children's future.

Telephone groups are now emerging as a resource for those who find it hard to have face-to-face contact in support networks [Wiener et al. 1993]. People whose symptoms have escalated in the end stages of AIDS do not always feel welcomed by or comfortable with healthy support group members. They may believe that their feelings about death and dying are too morbid or depressing for those recently diagnosed as HIV positive, and that other members will feel uncomfortable with wheelchairs, lesions, and uncontrollable coughing. Furthermore, even when transportation is provided, traveling to a support group can deplete the energy of those with advanced AIDS, limiting their ability to participate. Chapter 5 has a more detailed description of support group configurations and meeting topics after a child has been placed with a new family.

Food Assistance and Nutrition

Proper nutrition is especially important for individuals who are HIV positive. Because people living with HIV have weakened immune systems, they are susceptible to contracting food-borne illnesses, which typically result from improper handling of food. People with HIV/AIDS can experience prolonged and severe symptoms from food poisoning. They should be careful in buying, preparing, and storing foods and in eating nutritiously.

Child welfare agencies should seek out local community organizations that meet the nutritional needs of people with HIV/AIDS. Project Open Hand was the nation's first grassroots response to the nutritional needs of people with HIV/AIDS. Operated in California's San Francisco, Alameda, and Marin Counties, the program each day provides nutritious, home-delivered meals and groceries to men, women, and children living with symptomatic HIV and AIDS. Project Open Hand relies on a volunteer corps of 2,100 people to deliver and prepare meals. Agencies can contact Project Open Hand, 2720 17th St, San Francisco, CA 94110-1405, for a free replication manual.

Hospice Care

Hospice care provides health, homemaker, and social services in a home-like setting or in a facility for persons with a terminal illness, like HIV/AIDS, who have a life expectancy of six months or less. (Some programs extend this period.) These services are especially helpful in providing and monitoring pain-relieving medications and in coordinating medical resources for a patient 24 hours a day. Hospice care can also be an excellent resource for counseling and support for all family members and other loved ones.

REFERENCE

Wiener, L., Spencer, E.D., Davidson, R., & Fair, C. (1993). National telephone support groups: A new avenue toward psychosocial support for HIV-infected children and their families. *Social Work with Groups*, *16*(3): 55-71.

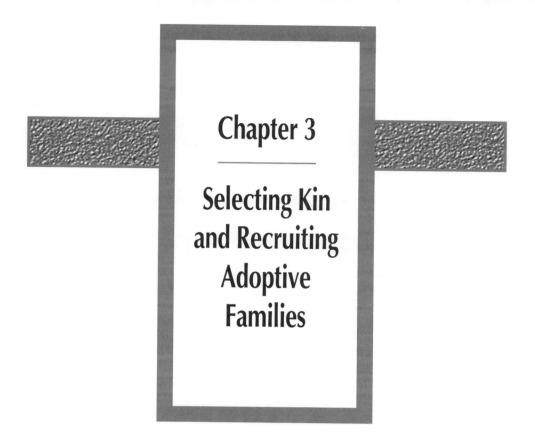

Chapter 3

Selecting Kin and Recruiting Adoptive Families

Child welfare agencies that identify kin and recruit adoptive families for children who lose their parents to HIV/AIDS must tailor their efforts to locate families to the special circumstances of the biological parents (if living), the children, and the extended family. Children awaiting placement may include:

- those who have living biological parents and will need a family at or near the time of their parent's death;

- those who have extended family members who will care for them before and after the biological parent dies;

- those who have been in family foster care and will have established relationships with foster parents when the biological parent dies; and

- those who are in out-of-home care and who will need new, unrelated adoptive parents.

This chapter focuses on the identification of kin and the recruitment of adoptive families for children whose biological parents are still living and anticipate the need for placement of their children upon their deaths. The tenets of this chapter, however, apply to families in other circumstances as well.

The populations of children listed above share the same needs for permanency in their lives as other children. However, a child's HIV status is not the only defining "special needs" characteristic for recruiting adoptive families and selecting kin. Other important characteristics of children that are relevant to the recruitment of families include age, race/ethnicity, sibling group status, developmental disabilities, and physical and mental health status. In addition, some of these children may have parents involved with the use of alcohol and other drugs and possessing other health problems. Some children may have been physically, emotionally, or sexually abused or severely neglected. All of these characteristics must be taken into account as well as the child's HIV status in developing and instituting recruitment efforts. Agencies should approach identifying kin and recruiting adoptive families with the philosophy that these children have a variety of unique strengths and needs, rather than focusing one-dimensionally on a child and/or parent's HIV status.

■ CHARACTERISTICS OF CHILDREN NEEDING PLACEMENT AND AGENCY PRACTICES

Children who lose their parents to HIV/AIDS share common characteristics that need to be considered in the identification and selection of future caregivers. Most will have special needs, will be part of sibling groups, and will benefit from services that concentrate on selecting or recruiting future caregivers in the communities where the children live and try to maintain cultural and ethnic group connections.

HIV-Affected Children as "Special Needs" Children

It is important to recognize that child welfare agencies will be recruiting for two different subgroups of children. The majority of children needing placement will not be HIV infected but will have a parent or parents and siblings who are HIV positive. The remaining children will be HIV infected. Whether or not the children are HIV positive, they share one common characteristic—they will be grieving the actual or anticipated loss of one or both parents. Many will also experience the loss of siblings. If they are HIV positive, they will most likely be dealing with their own feelings about living and dying. Because of these children's circumstances, they will need compassionate social services, and may also need mental health services.

Sibling Placement Issues for Children Who Are HIV Affected

Many of the children who lose their parents to HIV/AIDS will be part of sibling groups. While an agency should adhere to the practice of placing siblings together to the extent possible, it may be especially difficult with this population of children, since some will be HIV infected and others healthy. Children who are HIV positive require intensive medical services, emotional supports, and mental health counseling to help them deal with the cause of their parent's infection and their own prognosis. The new parents of children who are HIV infected will need to learn how to care for a sick child, and ultimately, how to deal with the child's death. They will especially need support services, including respite care and homemaker services, and such psychological supports as parent groups and counseling. (See Chapter 5.) Children who are not HIV infected may have different needs than their siblings, needs that may not be met because of the attention that must be given to their HIV-infected sibling.

In addition, child welfare agencies currently selecting kin and recruiting adoptive families for this special population report that many of the children in need of permanency come from large sibling groups of four or five children. The sibling group's size, coupled with the different HIV serostatus of related children, will impact the agency's ability to place siblings together. Other factors, like health, age, emotional needs, or other individual circumstances will further complicate such a placement.

Given the intensive care needed by an HIV-infected child, separation of siblings may be justified and necessary in some instances for all the siblings to have their needs met. In those instances, child welfare agencies should create opportunities through continued frequent contact and visitation to ensure that siblings remain emotionally connected with one another. Only families who will encourage and support sibling contact should be selected for these children. This is especially important because the children who are HIV infected are often the younger siblings in the family. Older children may have had an active caretaking role with the younger siblings, and the older children's adjustment will be affected by their ability to maintain contact with their young siblings.

Community-Specific Efforts

Since people with HIV/AIDS can experience long periods of illness followed by significant periods of remission, child welfare agencies should seek to identify kin and recruit adoptive families for these children in the same community whenever possible. When biological parent(s) live near kin or adoptive families, it is easier to: 1) schedule regular visits for children and their new family; 2) transition gradually into their new arrangements; 3) establish positive and supportive relationships with both sets of parents; and 4) have ready access to either set of parents, depending on the progress of the disease and the biological parents' ability to care for their children. It is likely that biological parents, children, kin, and adoptive parents will be intensely involved with each other for an extended period of time, so professionals should be prepared to discuss during the recruitment and selection processes (particularly with adoptive parents but also with kin) the implications of such intense involvement. Professionals may also need training in negotiation skills to help them identify main issues and find solutions acceptable to all parties, since these relationships will develop under extremely stressful circumstances.

■ IDENTIFICATION AND SELECTION OF KIN

Early in their work with biological parents who are HIV infected, child welfare agencies should explore the identification of kin to care for the children when the parents can no longer care for them. Kin have traditionally provided care for children when their families are in crisis. Both paternal and maternal extended family members, including biological fathers, should be explored as possible resources for the children. Factors that should influence biological parents' selection of extended family to care for their children include:

- willingness and ability of kin to care for the children;

- kin's financial ability to provide care and the availability of financial assistance;

- the health of kinship caregivers and other family members; and

- the relationships that exist within the whole family. A holistic model that recognizes the physical, spiritual, emotional, and cognitive needs of the children, biological parents, and extended family members should be employed in identifying and selecting kin.

Care by extended family members can support the family's sense of strength to care for their own, promote positive family functioning and self-reliance, reinforce the children's sense of identity and family history, and reduce the trauma a child may experience from the death of a parent or sibling. If agencies are unable to identify any extended family members who are willing and able to care for the children, they should actively recruit nonrelated families to adopt the children.

■ RECRUITMENT OF ADOPTIVE FAMILIES

Factors That Lead Parents to Choose Adoption by Nonrelated Caregivers

While many of the children who lose their parents to HIV/ AIDS will live informally with extended family members or be adopted by kin, many others will be adopted by nonrelatives, including foster parents. Various factors may influence a choice of nonrelated adoptive families instead of family members. These include:

- negative attitudes family members may have about HIV, substance abuse, and sexuality or denial of these issues, which affect their ability or willingness to care for the child;

- illnesses or disabilities among extended family members, for example, an overextended grandparent in declining health;

- substance abuse among the extended family;

- HIV/AIDS among the extended family;

- a history of child abuse or strained family relationships;

- discomfort with a family's cultural or religious beliefs; and

- legal realities, including custody battles, estranged couples, and the rights of biological fathers.

As noted, while extended family members should be assessed first and given early and serious consideration as permanent caregivers, agencies should anticipate that biological parents will not always want their children to be placed with relatives and that family members will not always be willing or able to take on parenting responsibilities. Among children who enter foster care and remain with their foster families for an extended period of time, a significant number may be adopted by their foster parents. If foster parents who have been providing satisfactory care for a child express interest in adopting the child and the child is emotionally attached to them, agencies should support this plan, so that the child will not have to experience yet another separation or move. All options for adoptive placement must be considered for these children—kin, foster parents, or new, unrelated parents. Also, agencies should work closely with the biological parents so they have a major role in the adoptive process.

Special Needs Adoption Practice as a Basis for Recruitment

Children and adolescents who lose their parents to HIV/AIDS reflect a new, emerging population with special needs. Child welfare agencies with special needs adoption programs are in the strongest position to recruit, place, and provide needed support for biological families, adoptive families, and children following placement. Because these agencies understand adoption practice, can identify community resources, and have placed children with many other types of special needs, they can adapt their programs to meet the special needs of children who lose their parents to HIV/AIDS. (See Appendix B for a list of selected agencies working with HIV-affected families.) Child welfare agencies with special needs adoption programs report fruitful collaborations with community-based AIDS service organizations to establish programs for these families. It is important for child welfare organizations with adoption expertise to be strong, early voices in communities about permanency planning and HIV/AIDS.

Degree of Openness in Adoption

For many children who lose their parents to HIV/AIDS, adoptions are likely to have a high degree of openness. According to CWLA [1988], placement openness refers to

> a process that is open and honest; one that supports the concept that all information, including identifying information, may be shared between biological and adoptive parents. The concept of openness, while protecting the rights of the individuals involved, should be an integral part of all adoption services. The degree of openness in any adoption should be arrived at by mutual agreement based on a thoughtful, informed, decision-making process by the biological parents, the prospective adoptive parents, and the child, when appropriate.

An open adoption is one in which, at minimum, the biological parents and adoptive parents share identifying information. Many adoptions also include various degrees of ongoing contact between biological parents (and others in their family) and their now-adopted children.

Both the advantages and possible disadvantages of open adoption should be discussed with biological parents, extended family members, adoptive parents, and children. As discussed in Chapter 2, an open adoption process can help biological parents overcome many of their fears about losing their children completely and encourage them to begin planning for their children's futures. When openness is a viable option, parents may be able to emotionally and physically involve themselves in the recruitment and selection of their children's future caregivers. For the biological parents who are living with HIV infection, the positives of open adoption may include the opportunity to keep in contact with their children and to build a relationship with the adoptive parents and peace of mind from knowing who is caring for and nurturing their children.

For the adopted children, the advantages may be several: not losing the historical link to their biological family, having access to information about their family's history and achievements, as well as ongoing medical information, and having psychological permission from the biological family to attach to the adoptive family. Open adoption may also provide children with an avenue to stay connected with kin who were unable to care for them upon their parent's death.

For adoptive parents, open adoption has been shown to frequently increase the emotional and physical closeness between themselves and their adopted children; to give them ongoing access to medical and social information about their children; and to reassure them that the biological family is also benefiting by having their children cared for by the adoptive family.

Problems that may arise with an open adoption should be thoroughly discussed with biological and prospective adoptive parents. For example:

- the biological parent may change his or her mind about the adoption;
- the adoption may be contested by a family member;
- the child's relationship with the biological and adoptive parents and extended family members may be divisive;
- the stress on the ill biological parents, especially during the final stages of the disease, may affect the adoptive family;
- potential class differences between adoptive and biological families may create uncomfortable feelings and situations; and
- the adoptive process may be long, stressful, and uncertain.

Sources of Adoptive Parents

Child welfare agencies will need to conduct targeted recruitment for adoptive parents with an interest in and commitment to children who have special needs. The following section outlines some potential sources of adoptive parents for both non-HIV-infected and ill children who lose their parents to HIV/AIDS. These sources include: (a) those who know the individual children; (b) those who have been personally affected by

HIV; (c) those who have already successfully adopted children; and (d) those with a particular religious commitment to serve those in great need.

People Who Know the Individual Children

Recruitment of adoptive parents should focus on those who know the individual children. Potential parents include relatives, teachers, nurses, doctors, respite care workers, coaches, troop leaders, foster parents, friends, and members of the biological family's religious congregation. Those who know the child as an individual are less likely to be deterred by the fear surrounding the HIV diagnosis because they are able to respond to the children emotionally and see the rewards in parenting the child. Some relatives who do not want to be considered as a resource for children while the biological parents are alive because of a history of conflict within the family may wish to reconsider their decision after the parent's death. The range of potential caregivers, beginning with relatives, should, however, be explored before the parent dies. Fathers and paternal relatives, in particular, should be thoroughly explored before adoption plans with nonrelatives are pursued. Reasonable efforts should be made to keep children with family and to respect cultural, community, and family ties. This is especially important to minimize the chance of contested adoptions after the death of the parent.

Individuals Affected by the HIV Epidemic

There is a second recruitment source for families: those who have been personally affected by the HIV epidemic, that is, who know someone who is HIV positive—a family member, friend, or acquaintance. Because of their personal experiences with HIV, they can relate to the whole child and not just the disease. They may have a special understanding or compassion for people who are HIV affected or infected and the ability to provide what these children need. Earlier experiences of specialized adoption programs regarding the adoption of children with Down's Syndrome provide a related example. These programs found that the families who came forward to adopt these children frequently had grown up with a brother, sister, cousin, or classmate who had Down's Syndrome. These families often focused on what a person with this condition could offer and felt they had a special understanding to offer a similar child.

Two groups of people have been greatly affected by the HIV epidemic—health care professionals and gays and lesbians. Both groups may serve as a recruitment pool of prospective adoptive parents. Many health care professionals, including nurses, hospice workers, doctors, and home health aides, have been at the forefront in caring for people with HIV/AIDS. They understand the symptoms and treatment of HIV and its related illnesses and have accurate information about transmission. Their knowledge and professional experience may increase their interest and capability to care for HIV-affected children in a sensitive and compassionate manner. Some health care professionals may be particularly interested in adopting children who are HIV positive; others may not because of their day-to-day experiences with HIV/AIDS.

The gay and lesbian population should also be explored as a source of potential adoptive families. Many gays and lesbians have lost friends and loved ones to HIV/AIDS. There is a strong desire in the gay and lesbian community to work in coalition on behalf of people with HIV/AIDS. Gay and lesbian individuals and couples, therefore, may be an excellent resource for children who have lost their parents to HIV/AIDS. Their similar losses may give them knowledge and strength to help children through the grieving process. At the same time, because the gay and lesbian community has suffered such a great loss from this epidemic, individuals who may not want to expose themselves to further loss may be unwilling to accept a child who is HIV positive. As with health care professionals, agencies should not assume that gays and lesbians will be able or willing to adopt these children.

Child welfare agencies have different practices and policies concerning gay or lesbian adoption. Depending on the agency and state law, this type of adoption may or may not be supported. Three myths often place pressure on agencies: that children will be molested by a homosexual adoptive parent; that children will become gay or be pressured to become gay if they are placed in homosexual adoptive families; and that children adopted by homosexuals will be living in an immoral environment [Sulllivan 1995]. A best first step for agencies to resolve this issue is to develop policy and practices on gay and lesbian adoption. CWLA [1988] recommends that "no single factor, including sexual orientation, should be the determining factor in assessing adoptive applicants." In fact, homosexual applicants for adoption should be assessed using the same—not different nor higher—standards as all other adoptive applicants. Too often in these adoptions, the emotional charge of the issues blinds people to the real issue—ensuring every child in need of a family a timely and appropriate adoption.

Individuals Who Have Already Successfully Adopted Children

Successful adopters, traditionally a valuable recruiting source in special needs adoption, can serve as excellent recruiting and parenting sources for these children. Agencies often find that prospective adoptive parents are referred by successful adoptive parents. The agency should also look to its recruitment pool of special needs adoptive parents. For example, if an agency has done a targeted recruitment campaign for sibling groups, adolescents, or children of color, some of these families may also be willing to consider a child who is, or whose parents are, HIV positive.

Individuals Motivated by Religious Convictions

Another recruitment source may be individuals with a particular religious commitment to serve those most in need or to minister to certain populations. Since the beginning of the AIDS epidemic, many, though not all, religious institutions and their leaders have been responsive to working with HIV-affected families. If possible, child welfare agencies should collaborate with their local AIDS ministry and other religious institutions to develop a strategy to recruit families for children who are HIV affected.

Child-Specific Recruitment

The same strategies that have enabled adoption agencies to place other types of special needs children for the last 25 years can succeed with these children. History demonstrates that if child welfare agencies make children visible in a caring and accurate manner, individuals will come forward to adopt them.

Various child-specific recruitment techniques may be employed in finding adoptive families for children who lose their parents to HIV/AIDS. Agencies will need to determine the most appropriate recruitment technique for each child as well as to look at the issues of confidentiality and disclosure for each child and his or her family members. In addition, agencies will need to be prepared to respond to people who inquire about specific children who may not have the best interests of the biological and extended family at heart. Recruitment techniques that agencies can explore include photo listing books; state, regional, and national exchanges; purchase-of-service contracting; media exposure; adoption parties; and One Church, One Child programs.

Whichever strategy is employed to recruit a specific adoptive family, child welfare agencies must work closely with the children and families to prepare them for recruitment activities, including photo listings and media exposure. For example, agencies can prepare older children for specific recruitment activities by informing them in advance about the schedule for a recruitment feature, helping them anticipate the probable reaction of classmates and others about photo listings and media exposure, and working with them ahead of time to decide how they can most comfortably respond to questions others may ask.

Photo Listing Books

Child welfare agencies may want to consider using local, state, or national photo listing books as a specific recruitment technique for this population of children, except in states with strict HIV confidentiality laws. Agencies routinely use photo listing books for children with special needs who are awaiting adoption and who need wide exposure to secure an adoptive family. Because of HIV-affected families' circumstances, agencies might consider placing photos of children with their biological parents in listing books, enhancing the openness of this type of placement. Agencies must also keep children's profiles updated and be willing to place them across state lines. The biographies developed by child welfare professionals must be sensitive to each child's individual circumstances, while presenting an accurate portrayal of the child's special needs. The confidentiality of the child should be protected, and only when there is an inquiry should the family's history with HIV be divulged.

Photo listing books are typically distributed to a wide audience of prospective adoptive parents through adoption agencies, adoptive parent groups, libraries, and individuals. Through these books, adoption workers and prospective adoptive families can link up with the child welfare agencies who have custody of the children featured. These books may be a viable recruitment technique for children who are HIV affected and who have been in foster care for an extended period of time, or for children who have

HIV/AIDS. Special provisions may need to be made for children whose biological parents still retain legal custody.

It will be important for agency staff to work with the individual children featured in photo listing books to explain that the purpose of the books it to help them secure a family of their own. It is also important to help them work through any feelings of embarrassment or loss of privacy when their personal history and pictures are circulated or feelings of disappointment if they are not adopted as a result.

Exchanges (State, Regional, and National)

State, regional, and national adoption exchanges can provide an array of services to agencies to make children awaiting adoptive families visible. These may include picture books, media features, adoption seminars, and adoption parties. Just as photo listing books do, adoption exchanges provide children who are awaiting adoption with wider exposure to other child welfare professionals and prospective adoptive parents. Policy exceptions may be necessary for children of parents whose rights have not been terminated.

Purchase-of-Service Contracting

For children who cannot be adopted through the above measures, agencies should contract for the purchase of adoption services through such specialized groups as the Family Builders' Network agencies, Tressler Lutheran Services, AASK, or specialized agencies within their state or region. (See Appendix C for a list of the Family Builders Network members.) These agencies specialize in finding, preparing, and supporting adoptive families for children who have severe special needs. Usually fees are paid by an agency only if a placement is accomplished. While the fee is often substantial, it is still far cheaper than years of foster care and offers a better alternative for a child.

Media (Television, Newspapers, and Videos)

Agencies should consider using various media—television, radio, newspapers, and videos—as a means of recruiting adoptive families. The use of media may be one of the quickest methods to provide public exposure to children awaiting adoption. On average, 60% of children with special needs who are highlighted in the media are placed with adoptive families. All media must be culturally sensitive and accurately reflect the racial, ethnic, gender, cultural, and religious diversity of the agency's clientele. Agencies should use the tenets and strategies for media campaigns outlined in Chapter 2 to develop child-specific media programs. Some agencies have found that media events that spotlight biological parents who are HIV infected making an appeal for families to adopt their children are also an effective recruitment technique, if the family is willing to do so.

Adoption Parties

In placing children who will lose their parents to HIV/AIDS with adoptive families, adoption parties may provide biological parents, children, and prospective adoptive parents with an opportunity to get acquainted in a nonthreatening environment. Children's circumstances will differ: some having lost their parents to HIV/AIDS, some whose biological parents have symptomatic or asymptomatic HIV infection, some who are HIV positive, and others who are healthy. Agencies need to take all of the children's circumstances and needs into consideration when planning adoption parties.

One Church, One Child

The One Church, One Child program, operating in 35 states, advises African Americans in church congregations about their role in providing adoption or foster care for African American children who need permanent homes. According to the national One Church, One Child policy statement on adoption, "agencies must use the resources required to recruit appropriate same race adoptive families" [One Church, One Child 1994]. In addition to targeting African American churches, these programs employ many of the recruitment techniques described above, including state, regional, and national exchanges, photo listing books, and electronic and print media. Because AIDS affects African Americans disproportionately, and over 80% of those who lose their parents to HIV/AIDS will be children of color, One Church, One Child may be an appropriate recruitment technique for many communities. Yet, at the same time, because AIDS carries a certain stigma and because some religious communities do not accept people with HIV/AIDS, some congregations may need to be educated and sensitized to the special circumstances of these families.

A collaborative partnership between One Church, One Child programs, local and regional AIDS ministries, public and voluntary child welfare agencies, and specialized placement agencies may increase the number of children adopted. The National AIDS Interfaith Network lists more than 2,000 local and regional AIDS ministries for people in different faith communities (Christian, Unitarian, and Jewish). These AIDS ministries, working with biological parents who are HIV positive, as well as extended family members, could unite with their local One Church, One Child program to make HIV-affected families visible to African American church congregations.

■ SPECIAL ISSUES

Caregivers Who Are Themselves HIV Infected

Agencies must be prepared to respond to situations in which the adoptive parents or kin caregivers for children who lost their biological parents to HIV/AIDS become HIV positive themselves. In some cases, agencies will find that the biological parent's choice of future caregiver or the person who comes forward to care for the child, either kin or unrelated adoptive parent, already will be HIV positive. Agencies may not, under the Americans with Disabilities Act, deny placement solely on the basis of an individual's HIV status. Agencies should, however, fully explore such issues as the child's previous exposure to loss and the standard of normal life expectancy in placement decisions, focusing on the best interests of the child. Special consideration should be given to the children's long-term security if the adoptive parents or kin are HIV positive.

Testing

Women and Children

Agencies should develop a clear and concise policy on HIV testing for all individuals receiving services: biological parents, children, and prospective caregivers. CWLA, a major national organization that has formulated HIV/AIDS guidelines for child day care, residential group care, and family foster care, opposes mandatory HIV testing of any particular group of individuals, especially children and pregnant women. (See Appendix D for CWLA's position statement on mandatory testing.) Instead, it recommends that agencies utilize an intake process that includes a comprehensive health assessment, one that indicates whether the child is at risk for HIV infection. A child is considered at risk for HIV infection if he or she or the child's parent(s) meet any of the following criteria:

- uses or has used IV drugs,

- has or had multiple sexual partners and engaged in unsafe sexual behaviors,

- engages or engaged in sexual activity with individuals who had been involved in risky behaviors, such as injection drug use,

- received blood transfusions before March 1985,

- has hemophilia and received blood transfusions or blood products before March 1985, and/or

- in the case of the child, was born to or breast-fed by its mother who was HIV positive.

If it is determined that the child is at risk of HIV infection and that knowledge of the child's HIV status would help in planning for the child's future, then testing is encouraged to allow for an early medication program. Testing, however, cannot be administered without the informed consent of the biological parent(s) or the legal guardian. Informed consent means that the person must be advised of the adverse consequences associated with the test. In the case of adolescents, state law may require that the adolescent give informed consent to the procedure. Agencies should consult their state's consent laws for these requirements. A number of states allow young people to consent to their own medical care (including testing) without parental involvement, if they meet certain criteria: they are runaways, homeless youths, or emancipated minors [Gittler et al. 1990]. When parental consent for testing or disclosure is necessary under state law but the parent is unavailable or cannot be identified, agencies should follow state procedure for judicial permission to test.

Agencies always should obtain written consent forms designed for HIV testing and disclosure purposes. Consent for HIV testing "is not covered by a general release form granting the agency broad health care decision-making authority, such as may be signed by parents when voluntarily placing their child in foster care." [Ryan and Emery 1991, 24]

An agency's decision to advise, request, or conduct HIV testing should be based on written policies that provide for the following:

- the reason(s) for testing must be based on concerns about the well-being of the child;

- pre- and post-test counseling within the agency or its service network must be available;

- there is a plan to cover the costs of testing;

- there is a plan for HIV retesting, when necessary;

- service plans must be developed for children and their families based on the testing results and with the involvement of the child's biological parents, legal guardian, adoptive parents, or kin, and when appropriate, the child; and

- there is a plan regarding how and under what circumstances the confidential test results will be discussed and disclosed.

A variety of tests are used to detect HIV infection in children. At the time of this writing, they are: the virus culture; the polymerase chain reaction (PCR); the p24 antigen assays; and the HIV Antibody test (ELISA). The Early HIV Infection Guideline Panel of the U.S. Department of Health and Human Services, Public Health Service, Agency for Health Care Policy and Research developed clinical practice guidelines for the evaluation and management of early HIV infection. For the diagnosis of HIV infection in infants and children, this panel developed recommendations presented in Table 3.

Because infants reflect their mothers' HIV status and the median time for maternal antibodies to disappear is approximately 10 months [European Collaborative Study 1991], the detection of HIV infection in infants is complicated. While the virus culture is the recommended test for infants, it is expensive, not widely available, and lengthy to use (results are not known for 28 days). The PCR test, as well, is not widely available. The p24 antigen tests are available but are less sensitive than the other tests. The ELISA test confirmed by a Western Blot is used to diagnose HIV infection in children over 18 months of age.

The results of the HIV test should be explained to the biological parents or legal guardian and child, as appropriate, and should be disclosed to others on a need-to-know basis. Foster parents and potential kinship or adoptive parents have a need to know such information to make an informed decision regarding their ability and willingness to provide ongoing care and support for the child. See Chapter 4 for a description of good practice and legal principles in relation to different forms of disclosure.

Adoptive Parents and Kin

As with children, there should not be a policy of mandatory HIV testing of prospective kinship and adoptive parents. An agency's decision to advise, request, or conduct test-

TABLE 3
Diagnosis of HIV Infection in HIV-Exposed Infants

AGE	TEST	IF TEST IS POSITIVE	IF TEST IS NEGATIVE
1 month	HIV Culture or PCR [1]	Repeat test to confirm diagnosis of infection	Repeat test at age 3-6 months
3-6 months	HIV Culture or PCR	Repeat test to confirm diagnosis of infection	Test with ELISA at age 15 months
15 months	ELISA	Repeat test at age 18 months	Repeat test at age 18 months
18 months or older	ELISA	Child is infected [2]	Child not infected [3]

Source: Early HIV Infection Guideline Panel (1994). *Evaluation and management of early HIV infection.* Washington, DC: U.S. Department of Health and Human Services, Public Health Service, Agency for Health Care Policy and Research.

[1] *If HIV culture and PCR are unavailable, p24 antigen testing may be used after one month of age.*

[2] *Diagnosis of HIV infection requires two sets of confirmed HIV serologic assays (ELISA/Western Blot) performed at least one month apart after 15 months of age.*

[3] *Confirmation of seronegativity requires two sets of negative ELISAs after 15 months of age in a child with normal clinical and immunoglobulin evaluation.*

ing of these potential parents should be based on written policies similar to those that guide the decision for any child. The adult's overall health status should be taken into consideration in assessing their ability to provide ongoing care to the child. As noted, agencies cannot deny an adoptive or kinship placement solely on the basis of HIV infection.

Confidentiality and Disclosure

Confidentiality and disclosure, matters interwoven with testing, are critical issues. Agencies must take them into account when developing strategies to select kin and recruit adoptive families for children who lose their parents to HIV/AIDS. The issues of confidentiality and disclosure need to be addressed from the perspective of the biological parents, children, kin, and adoptive parents.

Child welfare agencies should have a separate confidentiality policy that applies solely to HIV-related information. "The policy should comply with local, state, provincial, and federal laws, and affirm:

- the client's right to privacy and the agency's obligation to respect the privacy of both child and family, including the confidential nature of cases records;

- the need for informed consent to disclose information about HIV status; and

- a clear definition of who in the agency rightfully needs to know the HIV status of the family served" [Ryan and Emery 1991, 26].

The Client's Right to Privacy

Underlying confidentiality and disclosure are legal and ethical issues related to the right to privacy. Agencies have an obligation to respect the privacy of both the child and the biological parents, and as a general rule, should keep personal information, including the parent's or child's HIV status, strictly confidential. The duty to protect the client's privacy extends to the maintenance of confidential records that contain such information. The rights of privacy and confidentiality are particularly important in the area of HIV because of the discrimination that is often directed toward individuals with the virus. It may result in loss of employment and insurance coverage, difficulties in locating housing, and school problems for children.

The law of privacy draws on constitutional, federal, and state law. In addition, the right to privacy may be recognized under codes of professional ethics for certain agency staff members. These ethical standards may prohibit professionals from disclosing medical and psychological information regarding clients. An agency should consult its state law (and, if the agency receives federal funding, federal law) as well as relevant codes of professional responsibility to determine confidentiality requirements. These sources will provide general mandates as well as any exceptions that exist for HIV-related matters.

Even when there are no exceptions, the right of privacy is not absolute. It may be waived through informed consent to disclosure of HIV-related information. In addition, the right of privacy may be superseded under the doctrines of "duty to warn" and "need to know."

Informed Consent to Disclosure

An adult may consent to the release of information about his or her HIV status or the HIV status of his or her child. This consent must be informed, that is, the individual must be told and understand the potential consequences of the disclosure, and consent must be given freely. In some states, minors may consent to the disclosure of personal information about themselves. Agencies should consult state law to determine if minors may give consent to release such information, and if so, any special conditions that must be met. As with adults, when minors are permitted to give consent, it must be informed and freely given.

Need to Know

Decisions about who needs to know a child or parent's HIV status should be based on the provision of optimal care for all family members who are HIV infected and on the right of individuals who may be hurt by exposure to know of it. Those who may be exposed to HIV should be fully informed. In deciding who needs to know a child's or parent's HIV status, or both, agencies should consider whether disclosure will directly benefit the child or parent and whether it will affect the ability of adoptive or foster parents and social workers to help the child or parent. Individuals who may accept daily care responsibility for a child, such as kin, foster parents, or adoptive parents, must be told a child's HIV status before placement.

Because it is important for prospective parents to understand a child's circumstances, child welfare agencies should ask the biological parents to consent to sharing their HIV status with the prospective parents. While information about a biological parent's infection is not within the "need-to-know" principle, it may help the biological and kinship or adoptive parents to develop a more compassionate and understanding relationship; this would ultimately help the children to adjust to their family's situation. Child welfare agencies should work closely with kinship and adoptive parents on HIV confidentiality and disclosure issues during education and training seminars. Discussion of the biological parent's right to privacy and how disclosing may affect the reception of the children by extended family members, friends, and neighbors should be part of such training.

Agencies should also develop and adhere to a policy that limits the number of their personnel who know about a client's HIV status, whether it be the parent or the child. Agencies can lessen the number of staff who need to know by instituting universal precautions, developing confidentiality policies, and adhering to state HIV confidentiality laws. In all child welfare settings, agencies should implement and monitor their infection control and universal precaution procedures not only to minimize the number of staff who need to know clients' HIV status, but also to reduce the possibility of infection and to foster an environment perceived as healthful. Agencies should also develop clearly stated confidentiality policies so that personnel have guidance for respecting client information and disclosing it to others. These policies must also establish procedures for inadvertent or accidental disclosure and for the handling of records by all staff members, including secretarial support. Child welfare agencies should work with their legal counsel to review their state's most current HIV confidentiality law before making disclosure decisions. The content, implementation, and interpretation of HIV confidentiality laws vary by state.

The Duty to Warn

In some jurisdictions, courts have imposed a duty, under certain circumstances, to warn others that another person is HIV infected. This duty has been applied in situations where a professional has reasonable cause to believe that an identified third party is in imminent danger of contracting HIV. Because HIV is not contracted casually, the duty to warn generally will not apply to those who come in casual contact with a person who is HIV infected or to cases where the infected person is taking steps to protect the other person. Because duty-to-warn provisions vary significantly by state, an agency should:

■ discuss the options with the biological parent or youth in accordance with applicable state law and good casework practice, focusing whenever possible on the client's right to self-determination and his or her responsibility for informing others who need to know about his or her condition;

■ consult with the agency's multidisciplinary team, including a physician; and

■ consult with legal counsel. [Ryan and Emery 1991, 28]

Passive Disclosure

Agencies must consider the names they use in light of confidentiality issues. The names of agencies and programs that mention HIV/AIDS or "AIDS orphans" may inadvertently convey the HIV status of their clients. These names, in effect, may be a form of passive disclosure. These agencies should consider developing nonidentifying acronyms or slogans for their programs to protect the confidentiality of those living with HIV who may use their services. In adoption programs concerned with outreach to biological parents who are HIV positive and in recruitment of adoptive parents, the issues of passive disclosure require careful thought, planning, and policymaking.

Recruiting Adoptive Families and Confidentiality/Disclosure Issues

With regard to the issues of confidentiality and disclosure for the recruitment of adoptive families, child welfare agencies should consider developing both print and broadcast media to inform the public that *some* children in care who are HIV infected or affected are awaiting adoption. In fact, many of the media components described in Chapter 2 can serve as both an outreach mechanism for biological parents and a recruitment tool for prospective adoptive parents. If individuals come forward in response to such recruitment, where HIV infection is explicitly mentioned, then the issues of confidentiality and initial disclosure are diminished.

Some agencies may not be comfortable in indicating that the children needing adoption are HIV affected or infected. In public education recruitment efforts, agencies may therefore indicate that the agency is seeking families for children who are chronically or terminally ill, whose parents are, or both. If prospective adoptive parents are interested in these children, then they should be asked early in the recruitment process if they wish to be considered for a child who is either HIV affected or infected. This information, given without any name attached, will provide prospective adoptive parents enough information about a child or family's physical health to make a decision regarding whether to proceed with an application to adopt, but still maintain the biological family's confidentiality.

Whether in public education or child-specific recruitment campaigns, as soon as prospective adoptive parents have indicated their willingness to be considered for a child who is HIV affected or infected, in most states child welfare agencies are legally required to disclose a child's HIV status. While it is easy to focus on a child's illness, it is important to present the whole child and not just the disease. Child welfare agencies should share with prospective parents all that is known about the child and what they might reasonably expect to happen should they adopt a child who is HIV infected or affected.

In some situations, networking with other child welfare agencies to share information about available children can be an alternative to media recruitment, one that may reduce the danger of disclosure to the general public.

Working With Biological Parents

Regardless of the individual family's circumstances and the biological parents' feelings about disclosure, prospective parents must be told if the child is HIV positive as well as if the child has experienced the loss of a family member to HIV/AIDS. When possible, child welfare agencies should work closely with the biological parents to determine their level of comfort in disclosing such confidential information as a child's or their own HIV/AIDS status. Disclosure of confidential HIV/AIDS information to prospective parents generally reveals not only a child's status but also that of his/her biological parents. Even if a child is not HIV infected but only affected, a family member's HIV status may be unintentionally released. In addition, agencies may be confronted with identifying kin and recruiting adoptive families for children whose parents have not revealed their own illness to their children.

Many biological parents are in a unique position to recruit families to adopt their children—either among family members or outside the family. Parents, such as those who make an appeal through the media, may choose to give up their right to confidentiality because they want so much to find a family to care for their children. However, it is important that professionals help biological parents think through the negative reactions that may follow media exposure.

Subsidies

Subsidies for both adoptive and kinship caregivers are critical in the recruitment and selection of families for children with special needs, including those who are HIV infected or affected. Subsidies are an investment in families who adopt and kin who provide ongoing care for children with special needs, not an expense. If families know that subsidies are available, they may be much more willing to assume parenting responsibilities.

Adoptive Family Subsidy

Under Title IV-E of the Social Security Act, children who are placed for adoption may qualify for federal adoption assistance if they have identified special needs and either: (a) meet the eligibility requirements for SSI (Supplemental Security Income); or (b) were placed from the home of a parent or relative who was eligible for AFDC (Aid to Families with Dependent Children). Title IV-E adoption assistance provides monthly financial payments and automatic eligibility for Medicaid and Title XX social services. Federal law specifies that the amount of adoption assistance payment is to be determined through a written agreement between the adopting parents and the state that is based upon the needs of the child and circumstances of the family. However, the payment cannot exceed the amount of financial support the child would have received in a family foster home appropriate to his or her needs. By establishing flexible guidelines, federal policy anticipates that adoptive parents will assume an active role in negotiating a postadoptive plan of support for their child.

Children who are not eligible for Title IV-E adoption assistance may qualify for a state adoption subsidy program. State programs often provide two types of adoption subsidies: monthly financial assistance, commonly called a maintenance subsidy, and payment for medical, psychological, or other services not covered by Medicaid or health insurance, called a medical or service subsidy. A number of state adoption subsidy programs also provide Medicaid coverage to children who are determined to have a "special need for medical or rehabilitative care." (See O'Hanlon 1995 for more on addoption subsidies).

A number of Policy Interpretation Questions (PIQs), developed by the U.S. Department of Health and Human Services, Administration on Children, Youth, and Families, indicate that, contrary to what many people believe, a child does not need to be in the care of the state in order to be eligible for Title IV-E adoption assistance. However, many private agencies working to place children affected by HIV/AIDS with adoptive families report difficulty accessing adoption subsidies unless the children are in the custody of the state child welfare agency, which directly opposes the agency's intent of securing a permanent placement for children without having them enter foster care. As noted in PIQ 87-05, issued on December 17, 1987, children in the care of private agencies, SSI children, and certain relative adoptions are potentially eligible for federal adoption assistance. Since many of these children have special needs and come from large sibling groups, adoption subsidies are a critical element to secure permanency for these children. Child welfare professionals and advocates may need to work within their state to help broaden the interpretation and implementation of Title IV-E adoption assistance to include these children.

Kinship Care Subsidy

As with adoptive families, financial support of children placed with kin is a primary need of kinship families [Dubowitz 1990, Burton 1992]. State policies for the financial reimbursement of children in kinship care families vary greatly. Many states, for example, provide financial support to kin only if they are licensed or approved as foster parents. Other states prohibit the use of state and local funds to financially support children who are cared for by kin. Children not in the custody of the state who are living informally with kin generally are not eligible to receive foster care benefits. In many cases, however, they are eligible to receive benefits through AFDC (typically a smaller subsidy than that for foster care).

Subsidy policies related to children cared for by kin may make it very difficult for extended families to provide permanent care for these children—many of whom have special needs. The limited availability of such support raises a host of public policy issues for agencies serving children affected by HIV/AIDS. Child welfare agencies may respond to this issue by working to implement policies and practices that establish a uniform level of child welfare benefits for all children in the legal custody of the public child welfare agency. They can also work to ensure that children in kinship care have access to the various benefits for which they may qualify, including Medicaid, SSI, and child support payments [CWLA 1994, 56].

REFERENCES

Burton, L. (1992). "Black grandparents raising children of drug-addicted parents: Stressors, outcomes, and social service needs." *The Gerontologist 32* (6), 744- 751.

Child Welfare League of America (CWLA). (1988). *Standards for adoption service.* Washington, DC: Author.

Child Welfare League of America (CWLA). (1994). *Kinship care: A natural bridge.* Washington, DC: Author.

Dubowitz, H. (1990). *The physical and mental health and educational status of children placed with relatives.* Baltimore, MD: University of Maryland School of Medicine.

European Collaborative Study. (1991). Children born to women with HIV-1 infection: Natural history and risks of transmission. *Lancet 337* (8736): 253-260.

Gittler, J., Quigley-Rick, M., & Saks, M.J. (1990). *Adolescent health care decision- making: The law and public policy.* Washington, DC: Carnegie Council on Adolescent Development.

O'Hanlon, Tim. (1995). *Accessing federal adoption subsidies after legalization.* Washington, DC: Child Welfare League of America.

One Church, One Child. (1994). Program Brochure. Chicago, IL: Author.

Ryan, C., & L.J. Emery. (1991). *Meeting the challenge of HIV infection in family foster care.* Washington, DC: Child Welfare League of America.

Sullivan, A. (Ed.). (1995). *Issues in gay and lesbian adoption: Proceedings of the Fourth Annual Peirce-Warwick Adoption Symposium.* Washington, DC: Child Welfare League of America.

Chapter 4

Preparing Families and Children for Placement

This chapter focuses on specific issues that children, biological parents, adoptive families, and kin may experience during the planning and placement process. Before parents begin planning for their children, many have other urgent needs that need to be addressed—drug treatment, housing, or temporary financial supports, for example. In an effort to limit its scope, this chapter concentrates on specific permanency planning issues, but encourages professionals to identify and recognize the magnitude and complexity of parents' needs as they begin to plan.

Even when parents learn about an agency's program to help them make permanent plans for their children, they may not feel they need services. Professionals must be committed to work compassionately over time with parents who are HIV positive, going step by step, encouraging them to use the available services. In addition, professionals must recognize that parents' feelings about HIV, as well as the stage of their illness, will greatly affect how they respond to services and to planning. This section focuses on important aspects of working with parents who are HIV positive in helping them to make plans for their children. These include: (1) exploring permanency planning before they reach the end stage of their illness and dealing with parents' sometimes unpredictable behaviors, especially during the final stages of the disease; (2) telling children and others about the family illness; and (3) developing a plan for children's future care.

■ ■ ■

Exploring Permanency Planning

While this chapter focuses on encouraging parents to plan early, before the onset of their illness, child welfare agencies nationwide report that the majority of parents are seeking services when they are almost at the end stage of HIV disease. This delay poses a different set of dynamics for planning than would occur if preparations began earlier in the parent's illness. At the latter stages of their illness, parents, clinging to life, may not want what little power and control they have over their own lives taken away, or they may not have the emotional energy to plan for their children. They may frequently change their decisions about future plans for their children, making it even more challenging for professionals to help them develop a thorough, comprehensive plan that can be carried out.

Throughout their illness, parents living with HIV/AIDS experience a variety of intense feelings, including denial, devastation, guilt, and isolation. They may also feel anger and fear because of society's response to AIDS. Some parents may feel guilty because, as HIV disease progresses, they will not be able to care for their children; other parents are in such denial that they do not believe they will die. In some cases, denial may manifest itself by individuals not returning for test results, so they can hold onto a false sense of good health. Many of the parents' feelings can also be attributed to a life of pain, and are compounded when their children are also sick.

In responding to parents, child welfare professionals must recognize that it may take a long time to engage them in dialogue about planning for their children's futures. If parents who are HIV positive are in good health and if they have the opportunity to work through their feelings about their illness, they may feel comfortable in beginning to make plans for their children's future care. As indicated in Chapter 3, agencies should work with parents to explore the range of possible permanent caregivers, starting with consideration of extended family. Agency staff should convene a family meeting to discuss the options for children, family resources, and present or past family conflicts. Such meetings serve to reinforce family decision making in planning for the children.

Whether parents will choose relatives to care for their children will depend on such factors as the parents' relationships with extended family, willingness and ability of kin to care for children, their children's comfort and existing relationship with extended family, and the type of environment in which parents would prefer their children to live. These factors may lead them to choose nonrelatives to adopt their children, or, if their children are in family foster care and the foster parents have demonstrated an ability and willingness to adopt, to choose them as their children's permanent caregivers.

Biological parents experience multiple benefits from early planning. They can play an active role in the identification, recruitment, and selection of their children's future caregivers. They can also use the time between the development and implementation of a plan to build a relationship with the future caregivers. Their sense of empowerment may be heightened and their feelings of guilt and abandonment reduced when they know who will care for their children after they die. At the same time, planning may bring about family conflicts that professionals will need to help resolve.

■ ■ ■ ■ ■

Early permanency planning also has legal implications for the placement of children. In some cases, persons with HIV disease suffer from AIDS-related dementia—the deterioration of thinking, behavior, and motor skills. Because a significant number of persons die from Class IV non-AIDS, in addition to the 40-60% of AIDS patients who suffer from neurological problems, it is important for parents to plan while they are still considered mentally competent to help ensure that the plans they make will be upheld after their deaths. See Appendix E for a detailed chart on the stages of HIV infection.

While many parents living with HIV/AIDS desire to make early custody plans for their children, planning may be delayed by personal and external circumstances. One may be their level of emotional or physical energy. Another may be a parent's denial and fear of death. Parents' fear of maneuvering in the social service and legal systems, as well as their distrust of lawyers and social workers, can also affect their willingness to plan. So may the lack of legal services or their inability to afford them. While proactive recruitment of biological parents by agencies, as described in Chapter 2, will help to alleviate some of these difficulties, child welfare agencies will need to collaborate with other service systems to reduce the obstacles and effectively serve families. Child welfare staff need to provide these parents with a great deal of support, compassion, and encouragement. Professionals also need to recognize that not all parents will be able to participate in planning for their children. In such cases, the child welfare staff must be prepared to plan for these children upon the deaths of their parents or be prepared to support other caregivers who assume care for the children.

Contents of a Plan

The plans parents and agencies collaboratively make for children should include the following components:

■ an exploration of permanency planning options and a decision as to which option is the best;

■ a list of the support services needed by biological parents, children, and the new caregivers for the child (who may be kin or adoptive parents) and how those services will be provided;

■ a description of what financial assistance will be available for biological parents and future caregivers;

■ a description of any legal issues and how they will be approached in the future; and

■ documentation of the biological family's history, including parents' philosophies and values, which can be shared with children in the future.

Permanency Planning Options

A recent survey shows that of children in New York City who are HIV infected, a large percentage live outside their own homes. While 45% live with their biological parents, 16% live with relatives, and 33% live with unrelated foster or adoptive parents

■ ■ ■

[Nicholas and Abrams 1992]. These arrangements reflect the fact that children may already be in alternative living arrangements when their parents begin to plan for their permanent care. This long-term planning will depend on individual family circumstances, including current custody arrangements, and each planning option will have its strengths and weaknesses. Among the options that biological parents may wish to explore are standby guardianship, guardianship, adoption, and kinship care (legally formalized or an informal arrangement).

Standby Guardianship

■ *What is standby guardianship?*

Several states have recently passed new laws that recognize standby guardianship as a legal option for certain families. Standby guardianship laws allow terminally ill parents to designate an individual to serve as their child's guardian immediately upon the parent's incapacity or death. Parents are thus able to make a permanent plan for their children without giving up any parental rights during their lifetimes. Standby guardianship laws protect children from the uncertainty of custody determinations, while providing parents with peace of mind and a sense of control over their lives that is often lost in the face of terminal illness.

■ *What does the parent need to do?*

Depending on state law, standby guardians can be appointed in one of two ways. The parent may file a court petition for judicial appointment of a standby guardian or may complete a written designation. To file a court petition, the parent must first choose and notify the potential standby guardian, explain the situation to the court, and then document the triggering event for guardianship. Typically, statutes require the triggering event to be the parent's physical debilitation, mental incapacity, or death. The court will consider the petition and determine whether appointment of the standby guardian is in the child's best interest. Although the court may hold a hearing to rule on the petition, the petitioning parent may be excused if s/he is too ill to attend. Once the court grants the petition, the standby guardianship is established and will take effect when the designated triggering event occurs.

The standby guardian immediately assumes responsibility for the child upon notice that the triggering event has occurred. The standby guardian must file with the court documentation of the triggering event—the death certificate or a physician's declaration of incapacity or debilitation. If the guardian fails to file the documentation within the requisite time period, the court will rescind the guardianship.

When permitted by state law, a parent may complete a written designation of standby guardianship rather than filing a petition for judicial consideration. Most states dictate the form that must be used and the parent need only fill in the blanks. Forms may also be provided by local legal aid offices or other organizations assisting people living with HIV/AIDS. Essentially, the parent provides the name of the standby guardian and the designated triggering event. The parent then signs the designation in the presence of two witnesses, who also sign.

Under most state laws, when the triggering event occurs, the standby guardian automatically assumes provisional authority for the child for 60 days. During that time, the standby guardian must file with the court a petition for appointment as guardian. The petition must include a copy of the parent's written designation of standby guardianship and evidence that the triggering event occurred. The court will grant the standby guardian's petition for guardianship if it finds the appointment to be in the best interest of the child.

Child welfare agency staff should help parents to understand the advantages and disadvantages of filing a court petition or using a written designation. The major benefit of filing a court petition is that the parent can be certain that the guardianship has court approval. Court approval is particularly important if any difficulties are expected with the appointment, such as the other parent contesting. The major drawbacks associated with court petition are that individuals may be intimidated by the court system, deterred by the petition filing fee, and/or too ill to appear in court.

The written designation method of appointing a standby guardian is attractive because it is immediate and uncomplicated. The parent is not required to explain his or her choice of guardian. The parent can take home the form, think through the options, and fill it in upon reaching a decision. The major disadvantages of written designation are that, should the guardianship be opposed, the parent will not have the benefit of court approval of his or her choice and that the standby guardian will be required to file a court petition during the often stressful time following the parent's death or incapacity.

■ *Why is standby guardianship a good planning option?*
Standby guardianship laws respond to a number of planning problems unique to parents living with HIV/AIDS:

- People living with HIV/AIDS often experience episodic periods of severe illness interspersed with periods of relatively good health. Standby guardianships ensure that children will be cared for during periods of incapacity or severe illness, while enabling parents to resume care of their children when their health allows.

- Standby guardianship laws recognize the social stigma attached to HIV/AIDS. These laws acknowledge that parents may be reluctant to seek help from friends, family, or the legal system and afford them the opportunity to plan for their children in a quiet, unobtrusive way.

- Standby guardianship serves as an especially valuable tool for mothers who are HIV positive. These women, as statistics reflect, are less likely than other mothers with terminal illnesses to be able to depend on their children's father to care for the children after their death. Often, the father has no contact with the children, is HIV positive himself, or is not the mother's first choice of guardian.

- Standby guardianship provides parents with peace of mind because it allows them to make permanent plans for their children without relinquishing any parental rights until the point of incapacity or death. Other planning options, such as traditional guardianship situations, require parents to give up their parental rights at the time they appoint the guardian. Although parents may make custody provisions through wills or other testamentary instruments, their children's custody will remain in limbo through an often lengthy probate process and the parents can never be certain that the court will approve the guardian they have appointed.

- ■ Standby guardianship involves a relatively uncomplicated legal procedure and requires the expenditure of very little, if any, money. Parents can easily change their choice of guardian if they so desire.

- ■ Finally, standby guardianship facilitates an early start in the planning process and encourages parents to begin thinking about other forms of planning. For example, parents can select a guardian who they also want to be the adoptive parent or can select a member of the family who will provide ongoing care for their children. In these cases, the parent, the child, and the new caregiver will have the opportunity and time through the standby guardianship arrangement to build or strengthen their relationship. Where biological parents are unable to make early adoptive plans, standby guardianship arrangements will allow them the flexibility and extra time to decide about their children's future caregivers, while having a plan in place to meet their immediate needs.

It is important to note that standby guardianship is not a planning option for every parent. In some states, only when parents are terminally ill may they petition to appoint standby guardians for their children. In several states, the parent must state that he or she is likely to die or become incapacitated within two years. In addition, custodial parents must typically show that the other parent cannot be found, does not desire custody of the child, or is not a suitable custodian for the child. Finally, under most standby guardianship laws, parents whose children have been placed in the custody of the state child welfare agency may not use this option.

At the time these guidelines were written, standby guardianship laws were in effect in Illinois, Maryland, New Jersey, New York, and North Carolina. Several other states, including Georgia, Massachusetts, Ohio, Pennsylvania, Tennessee, Texas, and Wyoming, have proposed standby guardianship legislation. Several states were discussing legislative action.

Guardianship

Particularly in those states without standby guardianship laws, agencies may want to help parents make guardianship arrangements. Guardianship appointments allow parents to name a person to be responsible for their children until the children reach adulthood. A legal guardian can receive financial benefits for the children, enroll children in school, and consent to medical care. In most states, parents can either name a guardian in their will or petition the court to appoint a guardian. Guardianship arrangements may also serve as a precursor to an adoption or may be part of a formal caregiving arrangement with extended family members.

In some states, parents retain some of their rights after a guardian is appointed, including visitation. Parents and guardians, for example, can make an agreement that the children continue to live at the home of the biological parent until the parent is no longer able to provide care, or they can agree to joint decision-making. In other states, all decision-making authority and physical custody are relinquished. In many states, guardianship may negatively affect the biological parents' financial status. If a child moves in with a guardian, in some circumstances, financial aid (such as AFDC) might transfer with the child.

Care by Extended Family Members (Kinship Care)

Child welfare agencies should also discuss with the biological family their views about their children being cared for by extended family (kin). "Kinship care is the full-time nurturing and protection of children who must be separated from their parents by relatives, members of the tribe or clan, godparents, stepparents, or other adults who have a family bond with a child" [CWLA 1994]. Kinship care may be temporary or long-term, formal or informal. Relatives may be willing and able to provide long-term care for children without legal recognition of the relationship. Other relatives may care for the children before they legally adopt them.

Because HIV/AIDS disproportionately strikes women who live in lower income communities, families may not have the resources or ability to adequately care for these children—most of whom will have special needs. Agencies, giving kin first consideration to care for children whose parents are HIV positive, should therefore work with kin to increase their ability to care for these children.

"Parents and their relatives are free to arrange care by extended family for their children. Because parents have custody of the child, relatives need not be approved, licensed, or supervised by the state" [CWLA 1994]. In informal kinship care arrangements, children are not eligible to receive foster care payments. They may, however, be eligible for AFDC, child support payments, or benefits under the Supplemental Security Income (SSI) program. Children in informal kinship care do not have a recognized legal relationship with the family caregiver. Guardianship or adoption should be considered as a way to ensure that caregivers have legally recognized status as parents or guardians, including the right to secure medical care for the child, enroll the child in school, and give the child the general care that a parent is empowered to provide.

Adoption

Adoption provides permanent families for children who cannot be cared for by their biological parents and who need and can benefit from the establishment of new and permanent family ties. Children can be adopted by either relatives or nonrelatives. The rights of both biological parents must either be voluntarily relinquished or involuntarily terminated for an adoption to occur, and the adoption must be approved by the court.

Adoptive parents have the same legal rights and responsibilities for their adopted children as for biological children, including the right to custody of the children and the right to make decisions about the children's education, religious upbringing, and medical care. Adoption is a good and viable planning option for families affected by HIV when there is sensitive outreach to the biological parents; preparatory work with parents, children and the adoptive family; and pre- and post-placement supports.

Support Services

One area that child welfare professionals should cover in helping parents to plan is the extent to which support services are needed for themselves, their children, and their children's future caregivers. Biological and adoptive parents and kin will need a range of emotional, social, physical, and financial support services. These supports might include budgeting, counseling, drug and alcohol treatment, food assistance and nutrition, homemaker services, hospice care, housing, medical care, recreational services, respite care, special education programs in schools, support groups, and transportation. Some of these service needs—such as drug and alcohol treatment and housing—should be addressed *before* parents begin planning for their children. Child welfare professionals should help families decide which services they need and how they can access and best utilize them. (See Chapter 5 on the provision of postplacement support services.)

Financial Programs

During the planning process, child welfare agencies may find that biological parents and their children need various forms of financial assistance and that prospective caregivers will need financial help as well. Child welfare agencies should be prepared to link biological and caregiver families with appropriate financial programs and assist them with application procedures. These may include AFDC, Federal Adoption Assistance and State Adoption Subsidies, food stamps, guardianship subsidies, Supportive Housing for Persons with Disabilities (Section 811), Medicaid, Social Security Disability, Supplemental Security Income (SSI), and Special Supplemental Food Program for Women, Infants and Children (WIC). Title I of the Ryan White AIDS Resources Emergency Act identifies cities with the highest incidence of HIV; if a family lives in one of these designated metropolitan areas, there may be a myriad of additional services available, including transportation, food banks, and cash assistance. Agencies need to network with other community-based organizations to coordinate and deliver services. (See Appendix F for a description of these programs.)

Legal Issues

Child welfare professionals may find that many biological parents need assistance in identifying and attending to certain legal matters, including making a will and a living will, designating power of attorney, and making funeral arrangements. Parents should be advised to make a will that describes what they want to happen to their possessions and details the arrangement of their affairs upon their death. In some states, parents can also name a guardian for their children in a will. Parents may need help with custody actions, including guardianship proceedings or relinquishing a child for adoption.

Parents may be interested in writing a living will, which gives directions about a person's medical care in case there comes a time when he or she is no longer able to communicate because of an illness. Living wills allow parents to express their wishes regarding the use of life support systems and the prolonging of life when they are critically ill. Because in some jurisdictions living wills are not sufficient to support decisions related to termination of life supports or are not honored by legal or medical authorities, in any event, parents may need help to understand the legal requirements in their state, including use of durable powers of attorney for health care decisions and other matters.

Some parents may want to give power of attorney to someone they trust, bestowing the authority to make certain kinds of decisions, including the right to spend money in a bank account, pay bills if the parent is unable to do so, and collect public assistance. Child welfare professionals may also be asked to help parents make their own funeral arrangements and arrangements for their children, if they too are ill. Child welfare agencies should provide parents with legal assistance, either through staff attorneys who can help parents with legal matters or through a collaborative relationship with local legal aid agencies. In addition, many communities have attorney associations that provide pro bono services for people living with HIV/AIDS.

Documenting Family History

Child welfare professionals should work with biological parents to create opportunities for them to share their family's history, including their philosophies and values, with their children, and if they feel comfortable, with their children's future family, whether relatives or nonrelatives. The information shared may include their own memories of childhood, favorite things to do, favorite foods and family recipes, special family holiday traditions and activities, and their friends and extended family members; their religion; their culture; their medical history; and their personal and professional accomplishments.

Professionals working with parents who have HIV/AIDS may find that those who are able to share their family history feel happiness and a sense of relief, knowing that they expressed their love for the children and that their children will remember them and be able to carry on the family's history. In addition, children feel a sense of identity, pride, and connection when parents tell them about their family history and about their childhood. Family history can give children a sense of their cultural, ethnic, and religious heritage and help them feel closer to their own family and community.

When parents can share their family's history and invite the future caregivers to participate in their family's traditions, all concerned have a unique opportunity to develop greater understanding of and appreciation for one another. When kin or adoptive families have an understanding of certain family traditions and activities, they are in a better position to help the child maintain a sense of family and cultural identity.

There are many ways for child welfare professionals to help biological parents share their family's history with their children as well as with kin and adoptive families. These may include creating opportunities for them to:

- Spend quality time with their children, telling them family stories and doing enjoyable activities together. (Professionals may want to encourage activities in which biological parents, children, and the new caregiver families participate together as a way to form new attachments.)

- Write a letter to each of their children.

- Complete their family tree.

- Tape record their children's favorite stories so they can still listen to the parent when their parent is no longer available to them.

- Buy or make and put aside a meaningful gift to be shared with their children on a special day, such as a birthday or graduation.

- Make a video of themselves and other family members, friends, and children during such special events as birthday parties and holidays.

- Make a family photo album, labeling and dating the pictures and including pictures of the children with their new family, if appropriate.

- Develop a folder of the work that each of their children has completed (pictures, stories, school papers, report cards, letters) to be shared with them later.

- Develop a family life book, documenting the parent's personal philosophies and values and special times shared by family members.

For parents who are HIV positive, making videotapes can be especially therapeutic. They can say goodbye to their children and express their love for them. Videos, of course, have the advantage that they can be replayed. Child welfare professionals should offer parents the opportunity to videotape early on in their treatment, preferably before parents begin experiencing HIV/AIDS-related illnesses such as dementia, which typically occurs in the later stage of the disease. Whether or not to make a videotape, as well as its timing and content, are parents' decisions. Taylor-Brown and Wiener [1993] succinctly detail the videotaping process for other professionals to review with their clients, including the pretaping interview(s), the taping session, reviewing the tape, and sharing the tape with the surviving children.

In the videotape, parents may want to express to their children: 1) their love for each child; 2) the concept of death, specifically stating that they will not be returning; 3) feelings parents may have been unable to talk about before death; 4) assurances that children were not responsible for their parent's death, diminishing any feelings of guilt and rejection; 5) permission for them to feel both happy and sad; 6) especially meaningful memories of their time together; 7) cultural and spiritual beliefs; 8) the names of important people with whom they want their children to have relationships, including the people who will be caring for them and the reasons the parents chose them; and most importantly, 9) permission to become a part of and attach to a new family. Professionals may find that some parents will want to discuss their illness on the video-tape, while others will not. Parents should decide where they feel most comfortable making the tape. After the taping session, parents should be given the opportunity to review the video and to process the many emotions bound to surface while taping [Taylor-Brown & Wiener 1993].

■ PREPARING CHILDREN FOR A NEW FAMILY

For parents, telling both their children and others about their illness is likely to be a very difficult decision. It will likely affect how willing they are to seek help in making plans for their children and to involve their children in making such plans. The source of a parent's infection will also affect how they tell their children and how the disclosure is received. In working with parents who are struggling with this decision, it is impor-tant to understand the reasons parents may have for deciding if, when, and how to tell children about their illness. Table 4 outlines some of the usual reasons that parents decide to tell their children about their family illness, and Table 5 details some of the usual reasons for not telling.

Professionals can play a pivotal role in helping parents to develop a plan to tell their children. Parents may need help in determining the right time, at what age, and how much to tell each child. Consideration of children's ages, personalities, developmental levels, language abilities, vocabulary, presence of magical thinking, and prior experi-ences with illness, death, and dying is critical in helping parents to make decisions about telling. Professionals can also help parents anticipate and plan responses to ques-tions their children may ask when told of the family's illness. These include: Why did this happen to you? Am I the reason you got sick? Am I going to get sick? Does it hurt? Are you going to die? What will happen to me? and Who am I going to live with? Doka [n.d.] points out that the questions children ask are a good indicator of what they are ready to hear, and that parents should listen for any underlying sensitivities in the questions that reflect that children are blaming themselves for the illness. Professionals can help parents by serving as a sounding board for those who want to practice telling with a trusted person.

Affirming the principles of honesty and openness, Doka [n.d] outlines guidelines for communicating with children about illness. These eight guiding principles are:

1. **Begin on the child's level.** Tailor the message to the child's developmental level, age, vocabulary, and experiences.

2. **Let the children's questions guide.** Give some basic information and then let the children's questions guide the communication. The response to the children's ques-tions should be open ended, and death should be described in jargon-free language.

TABLE 4
Reasons Parents Tell Their Children and Others That They Are HIV Positive

1. The burden of keeping a secret from their children, families, and friends is often difficult, stressful, lonely, and painful.

2. Children, family, and friends can help them cope with the physical and emotional stresses of the illness.

3. Children often know when things are not okay, and may start imagining the worst.

4. Children and other relatives may feel isolated from the family if they do not know what is happening.

5. Parents are afraid that their children and other family members may resent them if they are not told about their parent's illness, especially if the children are ill too.

6. When children receive accurate information about their parent's illness, it can open the lines of communication between family members, helping them find strategies to cope with their family situation, giving children the freedom to openly express their feelings, and perhaps helping brothers and sisters become closer emotionally.

7. Parents want to be the ones to tell their children, families, and friends about their illness before someone else does.

8. Parents want their children to understand how they became HIV infected so that they will be better able to avoid becoming ill themselves.

9. Parents are afraid that their children will blame themselves for the changes they sense around them.

10. Parents don't want their children to feel distrustful of family members.

11. If a child does not have the opportunity to help care for his/her ill parents, the child may not feel he or she had an adequate opportunity to share his or her feelings with the parent and the parent's death will come as a shock.

12. If their child is also ill, he or she may also have to participate in a treatment program and will need to understand the immediate effects of the illness on the family.

---

3. **Use the child's natural expressive means to stimulate dialogue.** Use stories, games, art, play, or other comfortable approaches as ways for children to communicate.

4. **Provide opportunities for the child to openly express feelings.** Because children's feelings vary during periods of family illness, they need a comfortable atmosphere to express their feelings.

5. **Share faith.** Expressed in either religious beliefs or philosophical reflections, faith can help children cope with difficult family situations.

6. **Encourage feedback.** Children should be encouraged and given the opportunity to replay what they heard as a way of clarifying misunderstandings.

TABLE 5
Reasons Parents Do Not Tell Their Children and Others That They Are HIV Positive

1. They don't know what words to use, how to say it, and when it is appropriate to do so.

2. They are anxious about how those they tell will respond.

3. They worry they may lose the support or respect of their children, family, and friends.

4. They feel that the information may hurt their children.

5. They are afraid that the people they tell, especially children, will unintentionally tell others.

6. They are concerned that if some of their children are ill while others are not, siblings may compete for physical and emotional attention.

7. They worry that their children will be rejected, discriminated against, and treated unfairly by others, especially if the children are also ill.

8. They fear others may make assumptions about their children, including the assumption that the children are also ill.

9. They fear they will lose the right to their children if they are sick and isolated.

7. **Utilize other resources.** Books, films, and support groups are among the resources that may help a child cope.

8. **Explain visits and medical procedures.** Children should be informed about visiting the ill family member and told how the person feels, looks, and responds. After hearing this information, children should be permitted to decide whether or not they want to visit.

Professionals may find that parents who are uncomfortable telling their children specifically about HIV/AIDS may be able to tell their children that they have a life-threatening illness. While it is each parent's individual decision, the professional literature weighs heavily on the side of telling children about the family's illness. With particular attention to long-term planning for children, telling children may help facilitate their moving into a new family. When children have a fuller understanding of the family's situation, they are better prepared for and able to participate in the transition to a new family and better able to explore their feelings of separation and loss. While it may be difficult for parents to tell their children's prospective caregivers about their illness, telling may help forge a strong attachment among all concerned and will give the prospective parents vital information, which can help them to understand the children's feelings. The prospective caregivers also may provide support to the sick parent.

■ ■ ■

Children's Understandings of and Reactions to Family Illness

To prepare children for their new families, professionals need to help children with various issues. One of these is understanding and coping with the illness. Children's reactions will depend on their age and developmental level. Table 6 details how children at different ages may respond and react.

Whatever children are feeling, they may not always talk about or show their emotions. Children will need opportunities through counseling and play and art therapy groups to express their feelings of abandonment, loss, grief, anger, and confusion. A child whose sibling is ill and receiving a great deal of attention may feel ignored and resentful and, at the same time, feel guilty. Children of all ages also need to be assured that the illness is not their fault.

■ PREPARING FAMILIES FOR PLACEMENT

Prospective Caregivers

Prospective caregivers need the opportunity to participate in an orientation meeting where they can learn about an agency's program and have their questions answered. When prospective parents decide to move toward placement, the agency should conduct a home study to assess the family's ability and willingness to provide an ongoing, caring, and loving environment. The placement process helps the family and the agency to mutually determine the types of situations the family could handle. Issues that should be covered include:

- the prospective family's own family history (including their current living situation, employment status, and parenting styles);
- the number, ages, and type of children they could parent and the types of needs to which they feel they can respond;
- their willingness and ability to parent a child with special needs and a child with a life-threatening illness;
- their willingness and ability to maintain a relationship with a biological parent for an unknown length of time;
- their interest, willingness, ability, and the length of time they could co-parent children affected by HIV/AIDS; and
- their comfort with and commitment to continue contact between siblings and extended family networks for children who are placed in different families.

Once prospective families have made a joint decision with the agency to proceed toward placement, they should be invited to participate in more intensive preparation activities. The preparation process should focus on caring for children who have lost or will lose their parents to HIV/AIDS and developing and maintaining a positive relationship with biological parents. Issues that should be addressed include:

- the medical aspects of HIV/AIDS;

TABLE 6
Children's Responses to Family Illness

AGE	CHILDREN'S RESPONSE
Children 4 years old and younger	Children 4 years old and younger may want to be near their parents at all times. They will need clear, simple, yet truthful facts about the family's changing situation. They may be upset if their daily routine changes. Parents should try to spend extra time with children, hugging and cuddling them. These children may not fully understand the seriousness of the family's illness nor the finality of death.
Children 5 to 8 years old	Because children are very vulnerable and sensitive during these ages, they may, in response to being told about their family's illness, hide their feelings and concerns, misbehave, show outgrown behavior (such as thumb sucking or bed-wetting), and ask many repetitive questions. They need their parents to give them correct information about the family's illness. They need to be assured that someone will take care of them. Like younger children, they will need to feel their parents' love. These children understand some aspects of death, yet may be confused by other aspects of what they are told. For example, they might not be able to understand how someone could be both "in a casket in the ground" and "in heaven."
Children 9 to 12 years old	At these ages, children may ask many specific questions about how their parents became ill, including questions about sex and drug use. It is important to give them correct information, but not more than they can handle. It is also important to provide children in this age group with information about the illness and its treatment. They may wish to take on some family responsibilities, but parents need to ensure that they do not become overburdened. These children may want the opportunity to have a say in who they live with when their parents no longer can care for them. While they typically understand the finality of death, they may not think young people and children can die.
Adolescents 13 years and older	While they may act "cool," mature, and independent, adolescents are particularly vulnerable to acting out their fear, anger, and grief regarding their parent's illness. Adolescents may try to gain attention through participating in risk behaviors, such as experimenting with sex and/or alcohol, tobacco, and other drugs. They may also act overly responsible and become too involved with their family's illness. Some radically change their behavior. It is important for them to find other teens they can talk to, because peer acceptance is crucial at this age.

- the developmental needs of children (both infected and noninfected children);

- separation and loss;

- attachment and bonding;

- grief and bereavement, especially ways to respond to grieving children;

- empathy for the biological parent and acknowledgment of personal feelings and biases an adoptive parent may have toward a biological parent's lifestyles choices;

- the shift in responsibility between the biological parent and new parent;

- discipline skills and the importance of alternatives to physical punishment;

- adolescent pregnancy and teenage sexuality;

- alcohol and other drug issues (AOD), including prenatal AOD exposure and managing a relationship with a chemically dependent parent;

- older child adoption;

- forming new sibling groups within adoptive or extended families;

- developing or strengthening relationships among siblings;

- negotiation and mediation skills;

- special challenges for adoptive and extended family caregivers (e.g., the dynamics of parenting young children at an older age, telling a child about his or her adoption at various developmental stages);

- legal permanency planning options, including adoption, standby guardianship, and guardianship; and

- agency practices and policies that affect the family.

Agencies should also consider including interactive sessions where biological parents who are HIV positive and kinship parents who are providing permanent care for a HIV-affected child can share their stories and talk about the importance of planning. These real life experiences can help prospective kinship and adoptive parents decide whether or not they want to and can parent a child with special needs as well as maintaining a relationship with an ill biological parent. Training modules developed in the area of special needs adoption can be adapted to include HIV/AIDS-specific issues.

During the preparation process, prospective families should complete the paperwork for foster parent licensing (if necessary), and in a few states, adoptive parent licensing. As indicated by Blanford et al. [1994], licensing prospective families is especially important when a parent dies before any legal arrangements are made. In such instances, the licensed family is able to step in and provide foster care for the child.

Biological Families and Children
At the same time agencies are working to recruit and prepare adoptive families and kin, they should work closely with biological parents to prepare them for placement.

Biological parents should be asked to develop a profile of themselves and their children. The Second Family Program of Lutheran Social Services in Illinois includes in this profile most of the following materials [Blanford et al. 1994]:

- a social history of each child;
- a description of each child;
- the children's medical records (documenting HIV status);
- the parent's medical records;
- a documentation of other family illnesses;
- each child's school records;
- current pictures of each child;
- each child's past experiences, losses, and behaviors;
- a portrait of each child's talents, interests, and habits, as well as other information to help the prospective parents know what the child is like;
- each child's psychiatric/therapy records;
- documentation of the children's legal status;
- documentation of any past history of abuse and/or neglect; and
- parent's religious preference for the children.

Prospective caregivers, including kin, need as much information as possible if they are to make an informed decision about providing ongoing nurturance and care for a child.

The Selection Process

In the Second Family Program, there is a sharing of information between the biological parents and the prospective caregivers. Prospective adoptive families are encouraged to develop a picture book that can be shown to biological families seeking a family for their child or children. The completion of the family photo book is also a good idea when children begin to live with extended family members, especially for those who may not know their relatives well. This provides biological parents and their children with a sense of the prospective family's life. Children in the prospective family should have the opportunity to participate in this part of the placement process, especially the older children. Upon the completion of the home study and family book, a prospective adoptive family is ready to be presented to biological families [Blanford et al. 1994].

When a biological family, with agency input, selects a prospective adoptive family from family profiles available to them, the agency meets with the selected adoptive family to share information about the HIV-affected family. The prospective adoptive family should be given the information put together by the biological family and then given sufficient time to decide if they want to meet the biological parents.

The first meeting between the biological and adoptive parents should occur at a neutral location, unless the biological parent's illness has reached a critical stage. This meeting helps the adults to learn more about one another and to exchange information. Only if the meeting goes well should the children be introduced to their prospective family. The agency should then help the families negotiate mutually agreed upon times for and frequency of visits.

Because this is a highly emotional time for both biological and adoptive parents, it is critical that both families receive support services from the agency during the selection process. The ability of child welfare professionals to mediate problems and negotiate solutions with the families is vital to a successful placement.

The Transitioning Process

Initial contacts with prospective future caregivers should occur in surroundings known to the child and, if appropriate, should be in the presence of the biological parents. These contacts will help the new parents to learn the family and child's daily routine and help the biological parents feel comfortable with their child's future caregivers. Positive communication between adoptive parents and biological parents will influence children's acceptance of impending changes. Preplacement or weekend visits over an extended period of time may ease a child's transition into a new family. In some instances, the transition may occur over a number of months, due to the biological parents' physical condition.

Children who are placed with another family before their parents' death are likely to have conflicting loyalties, and may feel guilt and anger. These children will be experiencing anticipatory grief for their parents and siblings and so may be unable to connect with their new family. But, when biological parents make plans early and implement them gradually, children are more likely to move easily into their new family. This transition period can help children to feel that their biological parents approve of their new family, giving them psychological permission to attach to the family and affording them the opportunity to get to know and adjust to their new family. Recreational activities, including family gatherings and holiday occasions, that include biological parents, children, and the new caregivers may be one way to help children transition to a new family.

■ SPECIAL ISSUES AND THEIR IMPACT ON FAMILIES

Separation and Loss

While separation and loss are core elements in any placement, the dynamics of separation and loss will be especially complex in these placements. Some biological parents may be afraid to make plans for their children, feeling that by doing so they may be prematurely separated from their children while they can still parent them. In such cases, biological parents need to be assured that they will retain control of decisions.

Fahlberg [1991] lists the following factors that influence a child's reaction to parental separation or loss: the child's age and stage of development, the child's attachment to the parent, the parent's bonding to the child, past experiences with separation, the child's perceptions of the reasons for separation, the child's preparation for the move, the parting and welcoming messages the child receives, the post-separation environment, the child's temperament, and the environment that the child leaves.

Early planning may help children to cope gradually with the anticipatory and actual loss of their parents. During the planning process, how a child, biological parents, and future caregivers are prepared for the child transitioning into a new home will significantly affect how the child copes with the separation or loss. According to Fahlberg [1991], the following factors should be considered: the attitudes of the individuals the child is leaving; the child's ability to express his or her emotions; the future caregiver's attitude; the message the child receives as he or she leaves a family, and the child's interpretation of such a message; how a child is welcomed into the new home; and the environment in which the child lives following loss.

During the different stages of their parent's HIV/AIDS illness, many of these children have experienced multiple moves. While children may not show a negative reaction to being separated from their parent, it is important for professionals and future caregivers to recognize that they may have difficulty forming attachments with others. By not attaching, a child is protecting himself or herself from the anticipated pain of future separation.

The stronger children's relationship with their biological parents and siblings, the greater will be their feelings of separation and loss. These may include feelings of rejection, loss of identity, and loss of control. Their sense of intimacy and privacy is also under siege. Other children may have positive feelings because they are getting a fresh start, especially children who feel as if they have been a burden to their parents. Rutter [1981] suggests that children between the ages of 6 months and four years experience especially intense emotional distress when separated from their parents, and this can result in less trust of caregivers.

Parents and professionals need to be aware that children respond to loss in individual ways that are shaped, in part, by the adults caring for them [Bowlby 1980]. Also, the length of time children react to separations or losses vary, but can last for years if they are not given permission or support to grieve their loss. Children must be given permission to have feelings and to express their emotions. Their feelings of separation and loss will often be expressed through such acting out behaviors as lying, stealing, fighting, or withdrawal. Each family is unique, and professionals must explore separation and loss issues based on each child's developmental stage and family situation.

Attachment and Bonding

The dynamics of attachment are likely to be profound in these placements. After placement, many children and their biological parents will want to have continued contact with each other. If so, it will be important for professionals and the new parents to create opportunities for them to do so, such as: 1) involving biological parents in helping to solve day-to-day problems; 2) participating in recreational activities and holiday festivities; 3) having regularly scheduled visits; and 4) attending children's medical appointments and school conferences [Fahlberg 1991]. This type of interaction will help parents and children feel they are important to one another, and can become the cornerstone for building a new extended family.

Most new parents will find it a complex and challenging task to establish a new family unit while helping children acknowledge and honor the loved ones they are losing or have lost. If the biological parents, children, and new parents have the opportunity to build a relationship, biological parents are more likely to give their children permission to attach and the new parents are more likely to have the authority they need to make decisions. In addition, if biological parents sense that their children are moving successfully into and attaching to their new family, their feelings of guilt and loss may lessen. These attachments need to be supported, for children's continued development as well as their sense of self and well-being depend on their ability to develop interpersonal relationships.

Children who have not resolved their feelings of separation may not be able to form new attachments. Bowlby [1980] indicates that new attachments are not meant to replace old relationships, and that a new relationship is likely to flourish when the new and old relationships are distinct. New caregivers and professionals should recognize that many children may be experiencing loyalty conflicts. Both new caregivers and biological parents therefore should support each other's roles in the child's life, promoting activities that can be done together and encouraging children to have relationships with the other set of parents.

Grief and Bereavement

Children as well as those kin caregivers or adoptive parents who have a relationship with the biological parents will suffer grief and bereavement before and after the parent's death. These individuals' attitudes toward death will be influenced by their cultural, social, religious, and ethnic histories and backgrounds, as well as by their relationship with the deceased. Grief, therefore, will manifest itself differently in each individual. Because society's overall response to people with AIDS has typically been hostile—ostracizing, rejecting, and isolating them—mourners may experience stigmatized or disenfranchised grief. That is, they may keep their feelings of anger, grief, and shame inside, because their right to grieve is not recognized.

Dane [1994, 19] indicates that sometimes surviving family members or the new caregivers decide not to talk about the deceased parent or circumvent traditional mourning rituals to avoid dealing publicly with the cause of death and its possible implications. This behavior can be detrimental to the child's grieving process; it fosters feelings of denial and shame—stigmatized grief. Children's relationships with the deceased parent will undoubtedly affect how they grieve. While the death of a parent is painful, typically the aftermath is more difficult for the children to endure, especially when they are unable to discuss their parent's death and celebrate their parent's life, or feel uncomfortable doing so.

Some children will transition into their new family before the death of the parent. This period can prepare these children for their parent's impending death, and may decrease the stress of bereavement. Because a child's process of loss begins before a parent's death, the transition from biological to adoptive or extended family must be made with great sensitivity.

In helping biological families grieve, child welfare professionals should look at family dynamics before the death, including their cultural, ethnic, religious, and social beliefs and how they influence their perspectives on death and dying. Families should be encouraged to discuss the death, express their grief, and thereby decrease the isolation they may feel from potential support networks. Children, especially, must have the opportunity to openly grieve.

REFERENCES

Blanford, C., Charles, P., & Mason, S. (1994). *Second Family program: One model for permanency planning with HIV-affected families.* Chicago: Lutheran Social Services of Illinois.

Bowlby, J. (1980). *Loss: Sadness and depression.* New York: Basic Books.

Child Welfare League of America (CWLA). (1994). *Kinship care: A natural bridge.* Washington, DC: Author.

Dane, B. (1994). Death and bereavement. In B. Dane and C. Levine, *AIDS and the new orphans: Coping with death.* Westport, CT: Auburn House.

Doka, K. (n.d.). *Talking to children about illness.* New Rochelle, NY: Graduate School, College of New Rochelle.

Fahlberg, V. (1991). *A child's journey through placement.* Indianapolis: Perspectives Press.

Nicholas & Abrams. (1992). The silent legacy of AIDS: Children who survive their parents. *The Journal of the American Medical Association, 268,* 3478.

Rutter, M. (1981). *Maternal deprivation reassessed.* London: Penguin Books.

Taylor-Brown, S., & Wiener, L. (1993). Making videotapes of HIV-infected women for their children. *Families in Society, 74,* (8), 468-480.

Chapter 5

Postplacement Support Services

Comprehensive child welfare services need to be available following formation of the new family, whether it be through adoption or through arrangements with extended family members. Because some children will be placed with families before their parents' deaths, the range and delivery of postplacement support services will, in many cases, look different from those generally provided to families after placement. When placing children who will lose their parents to HIV/AIDS, agencies should recognize that, in light of the biological parents' complex health needs and their feelings of grief and loss, they are likely to continue to need intensive support services after their children are placed with a new family. This chapter focuses on support services after placement for the new caregivers, children, and in some cases, biological parents.

In the past many agencies provided services to adoptive families from the time of placement until finalization. Once an adoption was finalized, agencies broke their connections with families. If a family needed support, it had to seek services in their community. Child welfare professionals have recognized, however, that the success of many adoptions depends in part on agencies providing an array of services to these children and their families indefinitely after placement. Not all agencies have the resources to develop postplacement services, but agencies can collaborate with other community resources to determine the extent to which the most critical supportive services are available, how they can best be provided, and who should take responsibility for developing, coordinating, and funding them [Watson 1992]. Postplacement services must meet the specific needs and circumstances of individuals and be an integrated part of the placement process.

■ COUNSELING

Continued counseling focusing on grief, bereavement, and separation and loss issues constitutes an important support service. When infants and toddlers are placed with extended or adoptive families, counseling may help the parents understand how young children express in behavior their feelings of separation and loss, during the transition into a new family, through crying, sleep disturbances, and regression in some developmental areas. Child welfare agencies may find play and art therapists an excellent resource in helping children work through their grief and other feelings. Latency-aged children are likely to need counseling that helps them to understand death. Since It is estimated that over half of the children who lose their parents to HIV/AIDS will be between 13 and 18 years old. These teens are likely to act out their fear and anger over their parent's illness, and will need age-appropriate services to help them manage their pain.

Kin and adoptive parents, especially those who have established a relationship with the biological parents, may also need assistance in working through their own feelings of grief and loss and the changing familial roles and relationships. Biological parents living with HIV disease who have placed their children may also need both individual and group support to help them cope with their terminal illness as well as their decision to place their children with another family.

■ RESPITE CARE

Permanent caregivers of the children who have been placed, whether adoptive families or kin, usually need respite care. This service allows the parents to attend to themselves or to other family members. Families caring for children with HIV/AIDS may have a particularly great need for respite care. Respite care services may free adoptive parents and kin to go to medical appointments; visit family members; attend to such household and family responsibilities as shopping, washing, and housecleaning; meet other personal obligations; and have some much needed rest and relaxation time.

Respite care services are provided on both a planned and an emergency basis. Agencies that offer respite care services should have policies that delineate the qualifications for respite caregivers, the details of service provision, and reimbursement arrangements. Agencies can provide respite care in four ways:

1. contracting with a professional home health care agency;

2. making formal or informal agreements with individuals, including relatives or close friends of the parent;

3. contracting with another social service provider that recruits and trains respite care providers; or

4. hiring, training, and assigning their own home health aides [Leake and Watts 1989].

When contracting with other agencies to provide respite care for clients, child welfare agencies are responsible for assessing not only the qualifications and training of the personnel but also whether the other agency's policies and service delivery are consistent with their own services and philosophy. Respite care needs should be reevaluated periodically to ensure that the care arrangements meet the individual needs of each family. Scheduling difficulties and the high turnover rate of respite caregivers may interrupt consistent care, increasing an agency's need to provide emergency respite care. Agencies should collaborate to develop a list of respite care providers who can deliver services on an emergency basis. Table 7 highlights the qualities, knowledge, and skills of respite care providers that foster a positive care arrangement for families. This list can be used by agencies to identify and evaluate potential respite care resources.

■ SUPPORT GROUPS

Support groups offer an open, nonthreatening social environment for people in similar situations to give and receive support; share feelings, hopes, and fears; and provide information that may prove helpful. Children and family members may benefit from attending support groups to discuss the broad range of HIV, kinship, and adoption-related issues after placement of a child. Support groups can be arranged for children, caregivers, or biological parents or a combination of these three. Child welfare professionals working with children and families should decide which would be the most beneficial support group format for them. Support groups by specific group configurations are described in the following pages. Appendix G details guidelines for support groups that can increase their effectiveness.

Group Configurations

Children Who Are HIV Infected

Children who have been placed with kin or an adoptive family and who are HIV infected need a nonthreatening place where they can openly and honestly express their feelings about HIV/AIDS—an environment free of stigma and discrimination. Since most people in these children's lives, including classmates, siblings, and kin, are not HIV positive, these children may benefit greatly from a support group. Such a group will allow them to share their feelings of anger, grief, and loss with other children who are ill and help them to confront the harsh realities of death and dying. Children who are placed with a new family may also find comfort from children in similar situations. Support groups organized by the Second Family Program of Chicago for children who

TABLE 7
Qualities of Respite Care Providers: An Agency Checklist

QUALITY	KNOWLEDGE AND SKILLS
Knowledge and Beliefs	Have the provider discuss his or her understanding of HIV transmission and disease characteristics.
Compassion	Have the provider describe ways to be compassionate and empathetic toward people with HIV/AIDS and their affected family members.
Availability	Discuss their availability, including evening and weekend hours.
Reliability	Have the provider demonstrate through references his or her sense of responsibility in providing care.
Team Player	Have the provider detail experiences where he or she worked as part of a team with agency staff and medical professionals to provide respite care.
Ability to Follow Instructions	Have the provider cite examples in which he or she rigorously followed instructions around diet and medical care for persons living with HIV/AIDS.
Trustworthiness	Ask the provider to respond to a case that involves HIV confidentiality and disclosure issues.
Ability to Handle an Emergency	Give the provider an emergency case scenario and ask for a response.
Health	Ask the provider for a full medical history to determine that he or she is in good health and free of any chronic infectious conditions.

Adapted from Leake and Watts. [1989]. Respite Care Guidelines for HIV-Seropositive Children. New York: Author.

are HIV infected and affected have successfully used art and dance therapists to help children understand their feelings and their family's situation.

Children Who Are HIV Affected

Children who are HIV affected and are placed with kin or an adoptive family may also feel anticipatory grief and bereavement, confusion, and anger. Children may feel guilty or jealous if their siblings are HIV infected but they are not. Support groups provide these children with the opportunity to share their feelings with other children who have also been placed with a new family. Children may also be confused and disturbed if they hear other people speak in a derogatory manner about their biological parents, siblings, or friends who are HIV positive, and they may need help in understanding what they hear.

Children Who May Not Know about Their Infection

In some cases, children placed with kin or an adoptive family may not have been told that they are living with HIV/AIDS. Some parents do not tell their children that they have a disease from which they can die, because they fear their children will become depressed, a state that can negatively affect the immune system and increase the chances for illness. They also want their children to enjoy life and have a carefree childhood. The St. Francis Center in Washington, DC, has a support group for these children called the HugClub.

Adoptive Parents and Kin

Adoptive parents encounter numerous issues when they adopt a child who is HIV infected or affected, and may benefit greatly from a support group. These parents may need support on ways to:

- develop or continue building a positive relationship with the biological parents and their extended family;
- maintain the family and children's confidentiality around HIV disease;
- provide care to children who are HIV positive;
- deal with possible discrimination;
- help and support their adoptive children in their feelings of separation, loss, grief, and bereavement;
- get help from other families on dealing with acting-out behavior; and
- create an environment where all family members have the opportunity to attach and bond to one another. Support groups can encourage more experienced adoptive parents to serve as mentors for newer adoptive parents, helping them with parenting skills and dealing with common parenting problems.

Kinship caregivers will need many of the same supports as adoptive parents if they are going to provide permanent, ongoing care for the children placed with them. In addition, kin may need help from others in defusing their feelings of anger and resentment toward the biological parents for contracting AIDS and for presenting them with one or more children to raise. Some extended family members may be the primary caregivers for the ill family members, and will need help in coping with stigma and discrimination.

Biological Parents

Biological parents who are HIV positive may need support from others after their children are placed with their new parents. They may need help working through their feelings of denial, isolation, anger, despair, and separation and loss, as well as anticipatory feelings about death and dying. Support groups may relieve their emotional pain and enable them to focus on the positive steps they have taken to ensure the welfare of their children. Biological parents may also want to talk about how their illness affects visits with their children.

Recurrent Themes of Support Group Meetings

Professionals may choose to plan some common themes for group sessions. For example,

Medical Care

New caregivers who are providing ongoing care for children with HIV/AIDS need to learn about medical specialties, terminologies, and protocols. Support groups can be an excellent environment in which to explain and discuss the significance of new studies about HIV treatment, seroreversion (the process in which many children born to HIV-positive mothers become HIV negative around six months of age or later), and testing. Guest speakers can supplement the medical information shared within the group. In groups, adoptive parents and kin may want to discuss caring for a child who is ill, explaining medical treatments to their children, and assisting the biological parent who is dying.

Resources

Support group members and leaders can share information about community resources, including support services and financial assistance programs provided locally. Group members can provide tips on how to access such services as respite care, homemaker services, transportation, and financial subsidies.

Talking to Children about AIDS

Adoptive parents, kin, and biological parents may need assistance in how to tell a child that he or she or another family member is HIV positive. This may be especially difficult for parents of older children, who will need to be told more details about the illness than a younger child. The appropriate degree of information to share with children depends on their ages, developmental levels, and language abilities. Kin and adoptive parents must know what and how the children have already been told. By using similar language and building on what biological parents have shared, adoptive parents and kin can lessen confusion for children. Individuals who have already told their children can share their experiences and offer suggestions for telling.

Anticipatory Grief and Bereavement

Support groups can be an important resource for children who are placed with a new family before their parent dies. Some of these children may be grieving the loss of physical contact with their biological parents, siblings, their old home, and their friends. Adoptive parents and kin who have developed a relationship with the HIV-positive biological parents may also be feeling anticipatory grief and bereavement. They too can benefit from an empathetic environment in which to discuss such feelings.

■ RECREATIONAL SERVICES

Recreational services, such as summer camps, family enrichment programs, and holiday activities, can create meaningful and happy times for children, new caregivers, kin, and biological parents after placement. These activities can support a kinship or an adoptive family as they experience change, grow, and develop as a family unit. Recreational services may also enable the new caregivers and biological parents to develop or enhance their relationship and support one another after placement.

Across the country there are a few summer camp programs that provide families and children who are HIV infected and affected with a stress-free and nurturing environment where they can relax, have fun, and share their feelings with other families whose lives have been touched by HIV/AIDS. Summer camp programs like St. Clare's Summer Camp and Camp Heartland, described below, are organized to provide such an environment, and are examples of a resource other localities might want to develop.

St. Clare's Summer Camp Program, administered by the AIDS Resource Foundation for Children in Newark, New Jersey, has 200 families in its summer program each year. This camp provides families with the opportunity to build memories through such activities as nature walks, swimming, crafts, basketball, fishing, boating, and cookouts. Time is allotted for camp participants to share their common experiences through support groups and stress reduction workshops. The Camp Heartland Project in Milwaukee, Wisconsin, offers camps for both children and families affected by HIV/AIDS. The camps for ages 6-16 provide children who are HIV infected or affected or those grieving the loss of a loved one from AIDS with the "opportunity to have fun, make friends, increase their self-esteem, and openly discuss their feelings about the disease" [Camp Heartland Brochure 1994]. Besides the typical summer camp activities, children can participate in night dances, pool parties, campfires, and carnivals.

Both summer camps have medical teams that include physicians, nurses, psychologists, social workers, and respiratory therapists specifically trained to work with individuals who are HIV infected. Both camps have training programs for volunteers, and enjoy the assistance of a dedicated group of people. Both programs accept children and families regardless of their ability to pay. See Appendix H for a list of summer camps in the United States.

■ SCHOOL SERVICES

School may be one structured, consistent environment for children affected by HIV/AIDS. If properly prepared, educational professionals can play a pivotal role in supporting children through periods of crisis associated with the death of a parent or a child's placement with another family. The various professionals who work in a school setting, including teachers, administrators, school social workers, counselors, and psychologists, will need training to understand the dynamics in these families. Properly trained school personnel may be ideally positioned to develop support groups for children affected by HIV/AIDS.

■ HOUSING

While some people with AIDS can qualify for federal housing programs and subsidies, when they die, their children and other family members do not qualify for these benefits. Transitional housing, which provides the family with time to find adequate housing after the parent's death, is critical for kin who are going to care for the children. Without transitional housing, children whose extended family has limited resources are likely to enter an already overburdened foster care system.

■ HOMEMAKER SERVICES

Homemaker services include having a paid person come into a client's home to prepare meals, do laundry, clean house, and, in some cases, provide transportation. Kin and adoptive parents caring for children who are HIV positive can especially benefit from homemaker services, especially when they are able to learn about the special dietary requirements of children living with HIV/AIDS. Their developmental and medical needs can consume a significant amount of time and interfere with parents' ability to attend to household chores.

REFERENCES

Camp Heartland. (1994). "Camp Heartland: A place to be accepted." (1994). Brochure. Milwaukee, WI: Author.

Leake and Watts Children's Home. (1989). *Respite care guidelines for HIV- seropositive children.* Yonkers, NY: Author.

Watson, K. (1992). (1992, Winter). Providing services after adoption. *Public Welfare, 50* (1), 6-13.

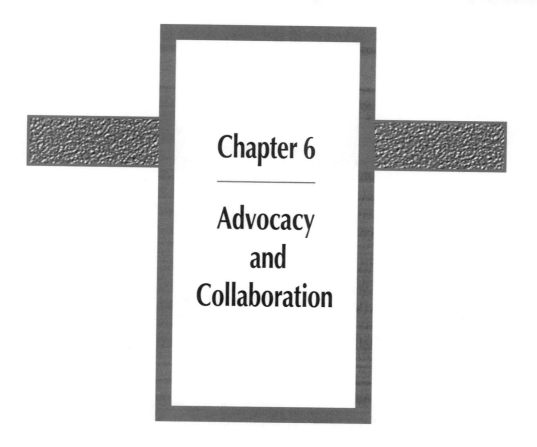

Chapter 6

Advocacy and Collaboration

F amilies affected by HIV/AIDS are an emerging population needing a range of core services such as housing and medical care; support services, like mental health counseling and support groups; and custody planning. Because their needs are so complex, service coordination and agency collaboration are essential. Child welfare agencies should develop collaborative relationships with health care providers, mental health agencies, community-based AIDS organizations, religious organizations, and other social service providers to help deliver coordinated services to both biological families and future caregiving families.

Multidisciplinary coalitions at all levels—national, regional, state, and city—are critical. These coalitions must work to ensure service coordination and collaboration and high quality services for biological families and new caregiving families both before and after a child is placed. Advocacy on behalf of families affected by HIV/AIDS is critical. Advocacy efforts, detailed in the following pages, are needed in five major areas (which correspond to the first five chapters of this guide): training, outreach and supports to biological families, selecting kin and recruiting adoptive families, preparing families for placement, and post-placement supports. In addition to these five major areas of advocacy, the pages that follow suggest directions for general advocacy and research questions to be answered.

■ TRAINING

Advocacy efforts are needed to:

- Ensure that adoptive parents, including kin who adopt, receive extensive training that increases or enhances their knowledge about HIV/AIDS and its impact on families.

- Ensure that comprehensive training is available to attorneys, social workers, and judges about HIV-affected families. This training must encompass the 13 components listed in Chapter 1 of these guidelines and focus on creating permanent placements for children through adoption and other arrangements, such as standby guardianship and informal care by relatives.

- Ensure that child welfare agency professionals working with HIV-affected families are able to participate in support groups that help them manage their feelings of burnout, helplessness, frustration, and grief.

- Develop risk-reduction education and prevention for adolescents living in families affected by HIV/AIDS.

■ OUTREACH TO AND SUPPORTS FOR BIOLOGICAL PARENTS WHO ARE HIV POSITIVE

Advocacy efforts are needed to:

- Ensure that high quality services can be provided to encourage biological parents to plan early for their children's future, framing early planning services as a prevention strategy that may reduce the numbers of children who will need foster care.

- Increase access to legal services for parents with HIV/AIDS, including assistance for expeditious custody planning and transfers.

- Ensure mental health support for children at the onset of the family's illness.

- Increase women's access to promising medical protocols and drug treatment.

■ SELECTING KIN AND RECRUITING ADOPTIVE FAMILIES

Advocacy efforts are needed to:

- Increase the availability and flexibility of adoption subsidies.

- "Modify existing confidentiality protection to allow limited nonconsensual disclosure of parental HIV status if such disclosure is essential to providing needed health and mental health services to that parent's child or children" [Geballe et al. 1995, 207].

- Increase the availability of the PCR test (Polymerase Chain Reaction) which is sometimes too expensive and not covered by insurance.

- Promote voluntary testing by professionals rather than home testing, to ensure that individuals receive the counseling and support they need and to help the nation track HIV/AIDS as a public health issue.

- Defeat federal and state proposals for mandatory testing of pregnant women and their children.

PREPARING FAMILIES AND CHILDREN FOR PLACEMENT

Advocacy efforts are needed to:

- Expand the use of standby guardianship as a legal mechanism to facilitate custody planning, by developing model legislation that states can adapt, crafting implementation processes, educating the court, and ensuring financial assistance for standby guardians.

- Revise child welfare voluntary placement policies so that parents can comfortably use voluntary placements for their children during episodic illnesses associated with HIV.

- Establish a uniform and appropriate level of child welfare benefits for all children in legal custody of a child welfare agency, including children in kinship care—one that meets children's physical, mental, health, and developmental needs [CWLA 1994].

- Provide financial assistance to guardians throughout the United States.

- Ensure that kin are considered first as potential caregivers for children who will lose their parents to HIV/AIDS, and then assessed for their willingness and ability to serve.

- Provide a comprehensive preparation process for biological parents, children, and future caregivers (either kin or adoptive parents) that encompasses issues of attachment, bonding, separation and loss, grief, and bereavement, as well as placement decisions.

POSTPLACEMENT SUPPORT SERVICES

Advocacy efforts are needed to:

- Create transitional services for future caregivers and children whereby, upon the death of the parent, the new caregivers and children do not lose such benefits as clothing, food, and housing that the HIV-infected parent received.

- Extend eligibility for and access to such services as respite care, family support, and mental health care from the child's biological family to all HIV-affected children and their new families.

- Ensure that such postplacement services as respite care, support groups, and counseling are available to new families for years after formation.

- Provide children placed with new families the opportunity to grieve and heal through such avenues as summer camps, support groups, life books, and videotapes of themselves with their biological families.

■ GENERAL ADVOCACY

Advocacy efforts are needed to:

- Ensure that the growing numbers of children and families affected by HIV/AIDS are a priority population for services and funding within the AIDS pandemic.

- Create a national database of programs, practices, and policies developed to help families affected by HIV/AIDS.

- Develop and provide case management services to biological and new caregiving families, including social service, legal, and medical specialists.

- Provide adequate and appropriate services for women and children affected by the epidemic in the cities identified by the Ryan White AIDS Resources Emergency Act as having the highest incidence of HIV/AIDS.

■ RESEARCH DIRECTIONS

Research, both qualitative and quantitative, is important to develop a better understanding of the family and cultural dynamics of HIV/AIDS, successful interventions, coping mechanisms, and the most critical services. Some areas of research that could inform the development or enhancement of child welfare practice, programs, and policy are described below.

- An estimate of the number of children who will lose a primary caregiver, whether it be mothers, fathers, kin, or adoptive parents, to HIV/AIDS.

- Projection of the number of children and families who will need child welfare assistance in creating permanent plans for children.

- Research on the psychosocial effects of HIV disease on HIV-affected children and kin.

- Analysis of children's reactions to family AIDS-related illnesses and deaths by their age, socioeconomic status, culture, and religious background.

- Examination of the factors that influence the HIV positive parents' timing of custody planning, including differences and similarities by culture [Geballe et al. 1995].

- Determination of the most critical support services for biological families before placement and for new families after placement.

- A description of the factors that influence the stability and cohesiveness of these new families, including coping strategies, interventions, and preparation processes.

- Analysis of the impact of long-term coparenting on children.

- Examination of the similarities and differences in children's grieving processes and coping mechanisms between children who know their parents died from AIDS versus those who were not told the cause of their parent's death.

REFERENCES

Child Welfare League of America. (1994). *Kinship care: A natural bridge.* Washington, DC: Author.

Geballe, S., Gruendel, J., & Andiman, W. (1995). *Forgotten children of the AIDS epidemic.* New Haven: Yale Press.

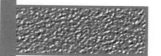

Appendix A

Subcommittee Members of the CWLA Task Force on Children and HIV Infection

■ **SUBCOMMITTEE CHAIR**

Terry Zealand
Executive Director
AIDS Resource Foundation for
 Children, Inc.
182 Roseville Avenue
Newark, NJ 07107-1619

■ **TASK FORCE CHAIR**

Donna C. Pressma
Executive Director
Children's Home Society of
 New Jersey
929 Parkside Avenue
Trenton, NJ 08618

■ **SUBCOMMITTEE MEMBERS**

Marilyn Barney
Director of Respite Care
Brookwood Child Care
25 Washington Street
Brooklyn, NY

Ellen W. Carey
Adoption Specialist
Children's Bureau
P.O. Box 1182
Washington, DC

Judy Cash
Executive Director
Children AIDS Network
 (CANDII)
222 W. 21st Street, F-116
Norfolk, VA 23517

**Phyllis Charles
Ramona Church**
formerly of Second Family
 Program
Lutheran Social Services of
 Illinois
6525 West North Avenue,
Suite 212
Oak Park, IL 60302

Kenneth J. Doka
Professor of Gerontology
College of New Rochelle
29 Castle Place
New Rochelle, NY 10805

Benjamin W. Eide
Ben Eide Associates
2568 NE 83rd Street
Seattle, WA 98115

Committee members listed have contributed actively to the development of these guidelines.

Aubrey Featherstone
Assistant Executive Director
Harlem Dowling-West Side
  Center
2090 7th Avenue, 3rd Floor
New York, NY 10027

Sandy Feldman
Assistant Chief
NJ Division of Youth and
  Family Services, Bureau of
  Licensing
CN 717
Trenton, NJ 08625

Ginny Foat
Executive Director
Caring for Babies with AIDS
P.O. Box 351535
Los Angeles, CA 90035

Elyzabeth Gregory Wilder
Kids Care AIDS Network
500 West 48th Street, #7
New York, NY 10036

Phyllis Gurdin
Assistant Executive Director
Leake & Watts Children's
  Home, Inc.
463 Hawthorne Avenue
Yonkers, NY 10705

Bruce J. Henry
Executive Director
Covenant House/New York
460 W. 41st Street
New York, NY 10036

Maryjane K. Link
10 Woodstock Lane
Pittsford, NY 14534

Debra McCall
Leake & Watts Services, Inc.
Specialized Foster Care
487 South Broadway
Yonkers, NY 10705

Sister Elizabeth Mullane
St. Vincent's Services
66 Boerum Place
Brooklyn, NY 11201

Robert H. Parrott
Children's National Medical
  Center
111 Michigan Avenue, NW
Washington, DC 20010-2970

Salome Peters
AIDS Coordinator
Baltimore County Department
  of Social Service
620 York Road
Towson, MD 21204-9968

Angela S. Rave
FaCT Project Coordinator
Maryland Department of
  Human Resources
311 W. Saratoga Street
Baltimore, MD 21201

Constance Ryan
Coordinator of Medical
  Consultation
Medical Support Unit, D.Y.F.S.
11th Floor, 1 South
Montgomery Street
CN-717
Trenton, NJ 08625

Paula Tarrant-Rivers
Administrator for Family
  Support Services
The Miracle Makers, Inc.
115/117 Ralph Avenue
Brooklyn, NY 11221-4011

Janet Thaxton
Deputy Executive Director
Boston Children's Service
867 Boylston Street
Boston, MA 02116-2601

Damaris Torrent
Council on Adoptable Children
666 Broadway, Suite 820
New York, NY 10012

Dottie Ward-Wimmer
Director of Children's Programs
St. Francis Center
5135 MacArthur Boulevard,
  NW
Washington, DC 20016

Lori Wiener, Ph.D.
Coordinator, Pediatric/HIV
  Psychosocial Support
  Program
National Cancer Institute
9000 Rockville Pike
Building 10, Room 13N-240
Bethesda, MD 20892

Jane S. Wimmer
Director, Tidewater Regional
  Center
United Methodist Family
  Services of Virginia
715 Baker Road, Suite 201
Virginia Beach, VA 23462

■ **CWLA STAFF TO
SUBCOMMITTEE**

Lisa Merkel-Holguín
former CWLA HIV/AIDS
  Program Manager
currently Program/Policy
  Analyst
Children's Division
American Humane Association
63 Inverness Drive East
Englewood, CO 80112-5115

Madelyn DeWoody
former CWLA Director of
  Child Welfare Services
currently Associate Director,
  Program Development
MSPCC
43 Mt. Vernon Street
Boston, MA 02108

Ann Sullivan
Adoption Program Director
CWLA
440 First Street, NW, Suite 310
Washington, DC 20001-2085

Cynthia Beatty
General Counsel
CWLA
440 First Street, NW, Suite 310
Washington, DC 20001-2085

Appendix B

Child Welfare Agencies Working with HIV-Affected Families, by State

I n March 1995, CWLA conducted a brief survey of 200 of its member agencies on permanency planning and HIV/AIDS to learn about agency programs and practices for HIV-affected families. Below is a compilation of agencies that wished to be listed as a resource to place HIV affected children with adoptive and extended families. Innovative programs known to the author that have not been contacted are also described and marked with an asterisk.

■ **ALABAMA**

*Children's Aid Society
Family Pairs Program
3600 8th Avenue S., Suite 300
Birmingham, AL 35222
205/251-7148
Contact: Teresa Cox Coker
Description: The Family Pairs Program provides support to biological parents who are HIV positive and recruits and prepares extended and adoptive families to care for their children.

■ **CALIFORNIA**

Los Angeles County Department of Children and Family Services
425 Shatto Place, Room 500
Los Angeles, CA 90020
213/351-5734
Contact: Eileen J. Ritchie
Description: This agency provides placement and other child welfare services for children through age 18 who are abused, neglected, or exploited, as defined by California Welfare and Institutions Code.

San Diego County Children's Service Bureau ■

Pediatric HIV Risk Assessment Team

6950 Levant Street

San Diego, CA 92111

619/694-5145

Contact: Glenyce Barber, Program Specialist

Description: The HIV Risk Assessment Program assesses and tests high-risk dependent children and consults with staff, foster families, and the community on pediatric HIV issues and chemical dependency.

■ FLORIDA

The Children's Home Society of Florida

Central Administrative Office

P.O. Box 10097

Jacksonville, FL 32247-0097

904/396-4084

Contact: Jean S. Price, Vice President, Social Services

Description: The Children's Home Society of Florida is a nonprofit agency with 14 offices throughout the state providing an array of abuse prevention and placement services for children of all ages and their families. It provides adoption services for children, including those who are HIV infected and affected, and has placed 28,000 children since it was established in 1902.

■ ILLINOIS

Jewish Children's Bureau of Chicago

1 South Franklin Street

Chicago, IL 60604

312/855-3754

Contact: Thomas Holmes, Director of Foster Care

Description: A Chicago metropolitan area child welfare agency, Jewish Children's Bureau is dedicated to the adoption of children with special needs.

*Lutheran Social Services of Illinois

Second Family Program

6525 West North Avenue, Suite 212

Oak Park, IL 60302

708/445-8341

Contact: Second Family Program staff

Description: The purpose of the Second Family Program is to promote the stability and long-term planning of families with an HIV-infected parent. It empowers parents to make decisions about their children's futures before they become too ill to care for them. Based on the philosophy of openness, the program structures a gradual transition for children moving from biological to adoptive families.

■ INDIANA

Pleasant Run Children's Home

1835 North Meridian Street

Indianapolis, IN 46202

317/924-5556

Contact: Harlene Swanson

Description: Pleasant Run Children's Home will accept children who lose their parents to AIDS in its therapeutic group home program if they meet other agency admission criteria.

■ MARYLAND

Maryland Department of Human Resources

Social Services Administration

311 W. Saratoga Street, Room 588

Baltimore, MD 21201

410/767-7523

Contact: Angela S. Rave, FaCT Project Coordinator

Description: The Maryland Department of Human Resources through the FaCT Model Project serves families affected by HIV/AIDS by developing permanency plans for children who will lose or have lost their parents to AIDS.

■ MICHIGAN

Spaulding for Children

16250 Northland Drive

Southfield, MI 48075

810/443-0300

Contact: Mary Lee Pearson

Description: All of Spaulding's permanency plans are tailored to the specific child, regardless of special needs.

■ MASSACHUSETTS

Lutheran Social Services

594 Worcester Rd.

Natick, MA 01760

508/650-4400

Contact: William Ames, Director, Youth & Family Services

Description: Lutheran Social Services is a private nonprofit agency available to provide specialized adoption services for children who lose their parents to AIDS. It offers supportive counseling to mothers regarding permanency planning.

Department of Social Services

HIV Parenting Partner Program
24 Farnsworth Street
Boston, MA 02210
617/727-0900, x560
Contact: Paula Arms
Description: Trained "Parenting Partners" are matched with an HIV-affected family and support that family through home management services, child care, respite care, fun activities, and possibly short-term foster care.

■ NEW JERSEY

Division of Youth and Family Services

50 E. State Street, CN 717
Trenton, NJ 08625-0717
609/282-1879
Contact: Constance Ryan
Description: When DYFS staff learn that a family is HIV affected, they refer the family to a community-based service provider, who, under contract with DYFS, offers an array of early permanency planning assistance, such as help identifying new parents, custody transfer, and living wills.

■ NEW YORK

Brookwood Child Care

25 Washington Street
Brooklyn, NY 11201
718/596-5555
Contact: Intake Coordinator
Description: Brookwood Child Care is a multi-service agency, providing foster care, preventive services, basic medical and dental care, and other support programs for children and families, including a specialized foster boarding home for HIV-positive children and their biological families.

Coalition for Hispanic Family Services

315 Wyckoff Avenue
Brooklyn, NY 11237
718/497-6090
Contact: Sonia Rodriguez; Julia Andino
Description: The Coalition is a community-based agency providing case management services, grief and bereavement counseling, foster care, adoption, support groups, and family-based treatment services.

Episcopal Social Services

18 West 18th Street
New York, NY 10011
212/675-1000
Contact: Elaine S. Rosenfeld
Description: Epsicopal Social Services places children who lose their parents to AIDS with permanent or adoptive families who are recruited and prepared by the agency.

Forestdale, Inc.

67-35 112th Street
Forest Hills, NY 11375
718/263-0740
Contact: Natalie Barnwell
Description: Forestdale Inc. is a private, nonsectarian, nonprofit agency which provides foster care and adoption services in the five New York boroughs and adjacent counties. It accepts referrals only from the Child Welfare Administration.

Ibero-American Action League

817 E. Main Street
Rochester, NY 14605
716/256-8900
Contact: Elisa DeJesus
Description: The League is a human service agency primarily serving the Latino community in Rochester with case management and support services to children and their families in the areas of foster care prevention, foster care and adoption, and developmental disabilities.

Jewish Child Care Association of New York

575 Lexington Avenue
New York, NY 10022
212/371-1313
Contact: Claudia Y. Williams, Ph.D., Foster Home Division
Description: The agency offers foster care, adoption, and permanency planning for families.

Leake and Watts Services, Inc.

Specialized Foster Care
487 South Broadway
Yonkers, NY 10705
914/376-0106
Contact: Debra McCall
Description: Leake & Watts Early Permanency Planning Project's main concept is to identify foster families for children of parents with HIV disease or other terminal illnesses who have not identified an individual to assume legal guardianship of their children. Family support services are offered as children transition to their adoptive home.

■ ■ ■

■ ■ ■ ■ ■

Little Flower Children's Services

186 Remsen Street
Brooklyn, NY 11201
718/260-8840
Contact: Kathleen M. Murphy
Description: Little Flower Children's Services maintains five Infants at Risk programs, which are specifically geared toward advocacy and placement of children affected by HIV/AIDS.

Louise Wise Services for Children and Families

12 East 94th Street
New York, NY 10128
212/876-4516
Contact: Nancy E. Cavaluzzi
Description: This community-based child welfare agency provides such services as emergency and specialized foster care, adoption and postadoption services, services for pregnant and parenting teens, independent living skills, parent skills training, adolescent group services, and preventive services for children and families.

*New York Council on Adoptable Children

AIDS Orphan Program
666 Broadway, Suite 820
New York, NY 10012
212/475-0222
Contact: Ernesto Loperena
Description: The AIDS Orphan Program provides supports to biological parents who are HIV positive and recruits and prepares adoptive families to care for their children.

New York State Department of Social Services

40 North Pearl Street, Floor 11-D
Albany, NY 12243
518/474-9433
Contact: Jean S. Felt, Bureau of Policy Planning
Description: The Department sets policy standards and provides supervision for agencies providing services for children placed in foster care and families affected by HIV/AIDS. The department offers statewide training and technical assistance on AIDS issues, including medical services, confidentiality, counseling, and assessment of risk and testing.

Society for Seamen's Children

25 Hyatt Street
Staten Island, NY 10301
718/447-7740
Contact: Cynthia Gindlesperger, Director, Foster Care and Adoption
Description: The Society has two separate units to work with children and families who are HIV affected, which advocate for biological parents and recruit adoptive and foster families for children.

The Children's Village

Dobbs Ferry, NY 10522
914/693-0600
Contact: Mona Swanson
Description: This agency offers residential treatment services, including individual and group therapy in grief and bereavement for boys ages 5-15, a foster boarding home, and an adoption program for boys and girls through age 16.

■ ### NORTH CAROLINA

Lutheran Family Services in the Carolinas, Inc.

P.O. Box 12287
Raleigh, NC 27605
919/832-2620
Contact: Stacy L. Smith, M.Ed., Director of HIV Placement
Description: Since 1990, this agency has recruited, trained, and licensed foster and adoptive families for children infected with and affected by HIV/AIDS.

Pediatric HIV Permanency Planning Program

Duke University Medical Center
Department of Pediatrics
Box 3499
Durham, NC 27710
919/684-8111
Contact: Amy Zimmerman
Description: This program is designed to forestall foster placement of children who are HIV affected and to assist biological parents in identifying and selecting future caregivers for their children.

■ ■ ■

■ OHIO

Office of Child Care and Family Services, Ohio Department of Human Services (ODHS)

65 East State Street, 9th Floor
Columbus, OH 43215
614/466-7884
Contact: Colleen Shillington
Description: ODHS provides public placement and adoption services through county branch offices and children's services boards located in 88 counties. ODHS focuses on recruiting and preparing families to care for children with special needs.

Toledo Crittenton Services

3151 Chollett Drive
Toledo, OH 43606
419/475-8681
Contact: Gloria C. Smith, Nursing Coordinator
Description: This agency provides HIV/AIDS education and counseling to children, adolescents, and their families.

■ SOUTH CAROLINA

South Carolina Department of Social Services

Post Office Box 1520
1434 Confederate Avenue
Columbia, SC 29202-1520
803/734-5670
Contact: Shirley McClerklin-Motley
Description: The Department places children who lose their parents to AIDS with adoptive and foster families.

■ VIRGINIA

*My Sister's Children

United Methodist Family Services of Virginia
715 Baker Road, Suite 201
Virginia Beach, VA 23462
804/490-9791
Contact: Jane Wimmer, Director, Tidewater Regional Center
Description: A collaborative project of the United Methodist Family Services and CANDII: Children's Aids Network Designed for Interfaith Involvement, My Sister's Children is an innovative, comprehensive, family-centered system of permanency planning services developed to find adoptive families for children who lose their parents to AIDS.

Appendix C

Family Builders Network Members

Children Unlimited, Inc.
P.O. Box 11463
Columbia, SC 29211
803/799-8311

Department of Health and Social Services
Division of Community Services
Bureau for Children, Youth and Families
P.O. Box 7851
Madison, WI 53707
608/266-3595

Family Builders by Adoption
1230 Second Avenue
Oakland, CA 94606
510/272-0204

Northeast Ohio Adoption Services
8029 E. Market St.
Warren, OH 44484

216/856-5582

Project IMPACT
418 Commonwealth Avenue
Boston, MA 02215-2812
617/572-3678

Project STAR
6301 Northumberland Street
Pittsburgh, PA 15217
412/244-3066

Spaulding for Children
16250 Northland Drive
Suite 120
Southfield, MI 48075
313/443-7080

Spaulding for Children
36 Prospect Street
Westfield, NJ 07090
908/233-2282

Spaulding for Children
710 N. Post Oak Rd. #500

Houston, TX 77024-3832
713/681-6991

Spaulding for Children, Beech Brook
3737 Lander Road
Cleveland, OH 44124
216/831-2255

Spaulding Midwest
1855 North Hillside
Wichita, KS 67214
316/686-6645

Special Needs Adoption Program
908 W. Broadway 8W
Louisville, KY 40203
502/595-4303

Women's Christian Alliance
1610-1616 North Broad St.
Philadelphia, PA 19121
215/236-9911

Appendix D

CWLA Position Statement on Unblinding Newborn Seroprevalence Studies and Mandatory HIV Testing of Pregnant Women

■ BACKGROUND

Both in the New York State legislature and in the 103rd United States Congress there were legislative proposals that would require states participating in CDC-sponsored HIV epidemiological surveillance studies of newborns to unblind the results and notify the parent, legal guardian, or state official responsible for the newborn of the results. Presently, the Centers for Disease Control and Prevention uses such surveillance testing to characterize disease patterns by time, place and person; to detect epidemics; to evaluate prevention and control programs; and to project future health care needs. The survey is not a screening nor part of any prevention or treatment program.

At first glance these seem like modest proposals. A number of prominent individuals and organizations have expressed their support for them without much more than a first glance. On close examination, however, they have serious drawbacks for infants, mothers, and society at large. The Child Welfare League of America (CWLA) opposes both the unblinding of newborn seroprevalence studies and mandatory HIV testing.

CWLA believes that there will be additional legislative proposals for mandatory disclosure of infant test results and mandatory HIV testing throughout the late 1990s. The following talking points delineate the reasons CWLA opposes such legislative proposals.

■ TALKING POINTS

- **An HIV-positive test result in a newborn does not necessarily mean that the newborn is infected, but it is a direct indication of the mother's HIV-positive status.** Because all newborns have their mothers' antibodies, they will test positive at birth. Over an 18-month time period, 75% of the children lose their mothers' HIV antibodies, and only 25% who tested positive at birth are HIV infected.

- **The unblinding of test results is equivalent to mandatory testing of women.** Informed consent is legally required for all medical procedures and epidemiological studies in the United States. Unblinding the test results and conveying information about HIV status without informed consent violates the right of women to give consent to medical testing for themselves and their children.

- **Unblinding the survey results would do nothing to reduce HIV transmission from mother to child.** The most effective way to prolong the lives of children being born to mothers who are HIV positive is to prevent the transmission of HIV. Clinical trial 076 shows some promise for decreasing perinatal transmission. The results show, however, that to be effective, AZT must be delivered to the mother antepartum (before birth) as well as intrapartum (during birth) and to the newborn during the first six weeks of life (beginning 8 to 12 hours after birth). While beginning treatment antepartum and continuing it postpartum reduces the risk of perinatal transmission of HIV by 67%, beginning treatment postpartum does not produce such results.

- **Unblinding the survey results will not reveal which children are truly HIV infected for treatment purposes.** While medical care for children with HIV has advanced over time, there are still some questions about the effects of treatment on children who are only carrying their mothers' antibodies. One main treatment is to administer PCP prophylaxis as soon as a newborn is thought to be HIV infected to prevent the onset of Pneumocystis Carinnii Pneumonia (PCP). However, since the effects of PCP prophylaxis on noninfected individuals are unknown, attempts to prevent the onset of PCP might be dangerous to the 75% of antibody-carrying newborns who are not HIV infected.

- **Unblinding the survey results will not enhance the access of HIV-infected children and mothers to treatment services, nor will it significantly improve the health and well-being of children.** Survey results alone do not give parents immediate HIV-related medical care to extend their newborns' lives. Instead of unblinding the results, a more effective strategy is to provide comprehensive and culturally-competent health care services: developing, enhancing, and expanding prevention, counseling, and treatment services for all pregnant women and children. Encouraging women to test for HIV early on in pregnancy can help health care providers to effectively plan prenatal care, including admission into clinical trials.

■ **When faced with mandatory testing, pregnant women may not seek the health care services they need, including both pre- and postnatal care.** Mandatory testing will push people away from the health care system. In fact, if women were offered the chance to test voluntarily for HIV, the majority would do so, provided that they were assured confidentiality. Voluntary testing empowers women to make their own informed decisions and would encourage them to access pre- and postnatal care services.

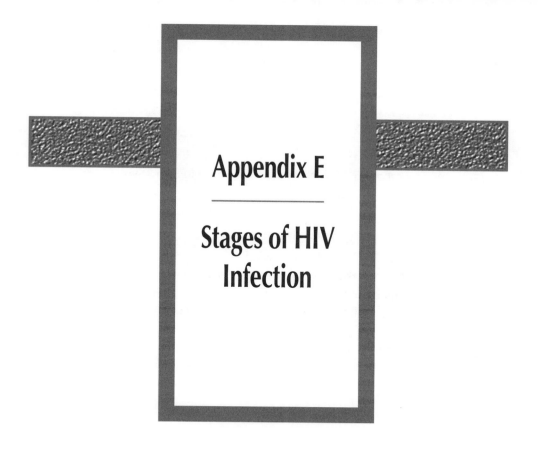

Appendix E

Stages of HIV Infection

1. *Acute Infection.* Initially infected individuals. The person may or may not exhibit flu-like symptoms. If flu-like symptoms are present they would be so mild as to be overlooked. There is a "window of nondetectability" (i.e., about 6 weeks to 3 months before laboratory tests can identify the body's defense of manufacturing antibodies to the invading virus). This is a highly infectious stage.

2. *Asymptomatic Seropositive.* Person looks well and feels well. Clinically, this stage begins when a positive antibody test has been received. This is also a highly infectious stage.

3. *Persistent Generalized Lymphadenopathy.* Symptomatic infection characterized by generalized lymph node infections. This is also a highly infectious stage.

4. *Symptomatic Disease.* Severely ill, end stage of HIV infection. Sub-stages A and B are not AIDS diagnostic criteria. Sub-C is clinical AIDS characterized by the opportunistic infections that make up the syndrome of AIDS. This is an infectious stage.

   A. *Class IV-Non AIDS.* Constitutional diseases: wasting syndrome, disabling weakness, and/or fevers.

   B. *Class IV-Non AIDS.* Neurologic diseases: encephalopathy, peripheral neuropathy, or myelopathy.

C1. *Infectious diseases diagnosed as AIDS* (i.e., Pneumocystis carinii pneumonia, candidiasis, herpes simplex virus, extraintestinal strongyloidiasis).

C2. *Other secondary infectious diseases* (i.e., oral hairy leukoplakia, multidermatomal herpes zoster, extrapulmonary tuberculosis, oral candidiasis).

D. *Secondary cancers* (i.e., Kaposi's Sarcoma, non-Hodgkin's lymphoma, primary lymphoma of the brain).

E. *Other HIV infections* (Chronic lymphoid interstitial pneumonitis, serious recurrent pyogenic bacterial infections).

Additionally, since 1993, CDC has included the CD4+ counts as indicative of AIDS. A count of 500 or more, a count of 200-499 (which may initiate prophylaxis for opportunistic infections), and a count of 200 or less (which calls for aggressive medical intervention) are merged with the clinical symptoms to establish a medical protocol for HIV/AIDS infection. The CD4+ counts are important to the initiation of specific therapies for HIV infection. Added to clinical manifestations for AIDS in women is invasive cervical cancer. Pulmonary tuberculosis and recurrent pneumonia (two or more episodes in a one-year period) have also been added to the list of trigger infections for AIDS.

Classification system developed by the U.S. Centers for Disease Control (CDC), 1986, and updated by CDC in 1993. The older system is used here because of its relative simplicity.

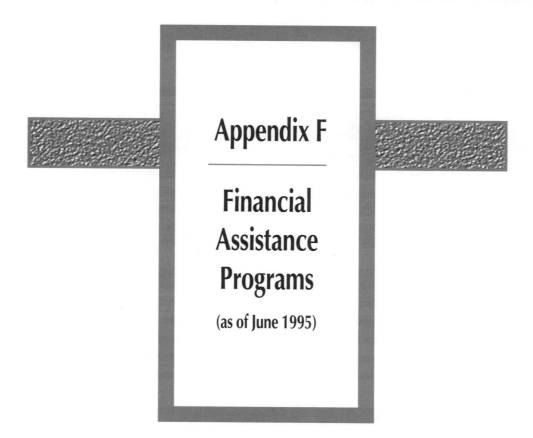

Appendix F

Financial Assistance Programs

(as of June 1995)

■ AFDC

The Aid to Families with Dependent Children (AFDC) program is the primary federal program to assist low-income children. The level of benefits for those eligible for AFDC is set by each state and varies from state to state.

■ FOOD STAMPS

The Food Stamp program improves the nutrition of low-income people by providing coupons or debit cards to cover part or all of a household's food budget. To qualify, households must have a gross income below 130% of the official poverty value of assets. The local welfare department should have information about this program, eligibility benefits, and application procedures.

■ HOUSING

In addition to possible assistance through rent subsidies, parents may also be eligible to participate in housing programs intended for people with chronic or terminal illnesses. The Regional Office of the United States Department of Housing and Urban

Development can determine if any of these programs are operating in a particular area.

■ Supportive Housing for Persons with Disabilities (Section 811) provides capital advances and rental assistance to nonprofit organizations to provide supportive housing for low-income people with disabilities.

■ Shelter Plus Care provides rental assistance and supportive services to low- and very low-income people who are homeless and have disabilities.

■ MEDICAID

Under Medicaid, the nation's current major public health financing program, states must provide services to certain groups of people, including those eligible for AFDC and children eligible for Title IV-E Foster Care and/or Adoption Assistance. Services covered under Medicaid include: inpatient and outpatient hospital care, doctor's services, diagnostic tests, skilled nursing care, home health visits, hospice care, and other medical services. Local social services departments have information about a state's Medicaid program and eligibility requirements.

■ SOCIAL SECURITY BENEFITS

People may qualify for Social Security benefits through a number of programs. For more information about any of the programs listed below or to apply for benefits, contact the local Social Security Office or call the Social Security Administration's toll-free telephone number, 800/772-1213. Some programs are:

■ **Social Security Disability Insurance (SSDI).** SSDI pays monthly cash benefits to disabled workers under age 65 and their dependents. Most people qualify for SSDI by working and paying Social Security taxes, earning credits toward eventual benefits. Adults who are unable to do any type of work are eligible for SSDI. In addition, children under the age of 18 may qualify, and children with disabilities who are age 18 or older may be eligible for dependents' benefits based on the earnings record of a parent who is receiving retirement or disability benefits, or on the earnings record of a parent who has died. The benefit level is determined by the amount of money earned while working (the "wage history"). Once someone has collected SSDI for 24 months, he or she becomes eligible for Medicare, a nationwide health insurance program for the aged and certain disabled persons.

■ **Supplemental Security Income (SSI).** SSI is a program that pays monthly benefits to people with low incomes and limited assets who are age 65 or older, or individuals of any age who are blind or disabled. SSI benefits, which vary by state, provide a monthly cash benefit up to a certain level. In 40 states, if you qualify for SSI, you are also eligible for Medicaid.

■ **Social Security Survivors Benefits.** If an individual worked, paid Social Security taxes, and earned enough "credits," then certain family members may be eligible for Social Security Survivors Benefits when the individual dies. Unmarried children under 18 (or up to age 19 if they are attending elementary or secondary school full-time), children who were disabled before age 22 and remain disabled, and stepchildren, grandchildren, and adopted children may be eligible for these benefits.

Estimates of SSDI, Survivors, and Retirement benefits that may be payable to an individual can be obtained by calling the toll-free number 800/772-1213 and requesting a PEBES, the Personal Earnings Benefit Estimate Statement.

■ WIC

The Special Supplemental Food Program for Women, Infants, and Children (WIC) provides food as well as nutrition screening and education to at-risk, low-income pregnant women, new mothers and infants, and children under age five. All WIC participants must have family incomes below 185% of federal poverty guidelines and demonstrate nutritional risk based on criteria such as anemia, inadequate diet, or abnormal weight. Participants are provided food packages tailored to their needs. In most states, participants are given vouchers that they may redeem at local grocery stores for such foods as milk, cheese, infant formula, eggs, cereal, juice, and peanut butter. Parents who receive WIC can also receive health and nutrition counseling to help them make good nutrition and health choices. The local health department has WIC applications.

■ FEDERAL ADOPTION ASSISTANCE (TITLE IV-E OF THE SOCIAL SECURITY ACT)

If children have special needs and are eligible for either AFDC or SSI (Supplemental Security Income), they may qualify to receive federal adoption assistance. Children who receive Title IV-E Adoption Assistance are automatically eligible for medical assistance through Medicaid. Federal policy requires that adoption assistance rates be based on a consideration of the needs of the child and the individual circumstances of the family. Each state reimburses adoptive parents at a different, individualized rate. The local or state child welfare agency has information about federal adoption assistance.

State Adoption Subsidies

Children who are not eligible for adoption assistance under the Federal Title IV-E program may qualify for state adoption subsidy programs. State adoption subsidies vary depending on children's needs and the state agency program. Usually, three types of adoption subsidies may be provided—medical, maintenance, and special service subsidies. Again, the local child welfare agency should be contacted regarding eligibility requirements.

■ FOSTER CARE MAINTENANCE RATES

Monthly financial assistance is provided to foster parents licensed by the state child welfare agency to reimburse them for some of the costs of a foster child living in their home. In some states, relatives or family members can receive monthly payments if they are licensed as foster parents or meet the required standards. Some states and counties supplement the basic foster care maintenance rate with additional funding for children with special needs. The local child welfare agency has information about foster care maintenance benefits.

■ GUARDIANSHIP SUBSIDIES

Only a few states have subsidies for legal guardians. A state attorney may be able to determine if guardianship subsidies are available.

Appendix G

Guidelines for Support Groups

Chapter 1 suggests guidelines for professionals who conduct support groups with people with HIV/AIDS. Similar guidelines will increase the effectiveness of support groups for HIV-affected children and their families.

To facilitate interaction between members, the size of a support group should be approximately 10 people, allowing members to feel like a group and providing them the opportunity to get to know one another. The actual number of members enrolled may be higher, since not everyone will attend every meeting.

At the first meeting, support group members should reach consensus on an open or closed membership policy, confidentiality procedures, and other ground rules. Group leaders may find that open or flexible enrollment (where new people can join the group at any time) may negatively influence group dynamics. Open enrollment may also impede group process and productivity, with members not feeling a sense of consistency or trustworthiness in the other members. If the group decides to have closed enrollment, the leaders should provide interested persons with referrals to other groups, and inform them of future open sessions.

The time, length, and frequency of meetings should be decided by the group and be convenient for all group members. The meeting schedule should be consistent, yet flexible, permitting the group to accommodate changes as they arise. Support group meetings can be held at such locations as child welfare agencies, clinics, public health centers, colleges, places of worship, hospitals, community centers, or parents' homes. Transportation and child day care, either in-home or center-based and onsite, are necessary services to enable parents to participate in support groups.

Leadership styles significantly affect the effectiveness of support groups. Support group leaders must have an understanding of group dynamics and the HIV pandemic and its effects on different populations, and must also be able to respond to members' questions and concerns about HIV/AIDS. Groups may benefit from shared leadership by different professionals, including social workers, health care providers, and spiritual leaders.

Leaders can use various activities to enhance the group meetings and make members comfortable with one another. For example, support group leaders, with suggestions from members, can invite guest speakers to the meetings. Possible guest speakers may include adoptive parents, pediatricians, nutritionists, early childhood specialists, and religious leaders. If members are interested, formal extended training can supplement the support group meetings, or members can attend additional training seminars. Groups can use films, videotapes, slide shows, and recordings to start discussions. Other activities and events, such as picnics and holiday parties, can strengthen group cohesion, while also providing members the opportunity to meet and get to know each other's children and families.

Appendix H

Summer Camps for Children with HIV/AIDS and Their Families

Camp Sunburst
148 Wilson Hill Road
Petaluma, CA 94952
707/769-0169

Summer Program of Herbert G. Birch
145-02 Farmers Blvd.
Springfield Gardens, NY 11434
718/528-5754

Camp Chrysalis
Waldo-Knox AIDS Coalition
P.O. Box 990
Belfast, ME 04915
207/338-1427

St. Clare's Summer Camp
ARFC
182 Roseville Avenue
Newark, NJ 07107
201/483-4250

Camp Heartland
4565 N. Green Bay Avenue
Milwaukee, WI 53209
414/264-6161

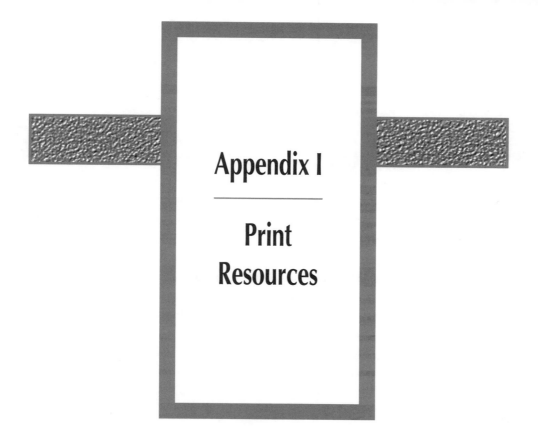

Appendix I

Print Resources

■ HIV/AIDS

The Gift of Goodbye, a workbook for children who love someone with AIDS, is a fine resource to help children explore their feelings and ask questions. [By Denise McKnaught; Bantam, Doubleday and Dell Publishing, 1993. To order: 2451 S. Wolf Rd., Des Plaines, IL 60018; 800/323-9872.]

Come Sit By Me is an illustrated storybook about HIV and AIDS. It is a gentle story about a kindergarten child with HIV and how the parents and his classmates deal with the illness. It includes brief but useful AIDS information and resource lists. [By Margaret Merrifield, M.D., and Heather Collins; Womens Press, 1990. To order: 7910 Woodmont Avenue, Suite 300, Bethesda, M.D. 20814; 301/654-6549.]

Be A Friend: Children Who Live with HIV Speak, a collection of writings and drawings produced by HIV-infected children and their siblings in therapeutic sessions, raises many of the issues of living with HIV/AIDS. [Edited by Lori Wiener, Ph.D.; Whitman and Co., 1994. To order: 6340 Oakton St., Morton Grove, IL 60053; 800/255-7675.]

How Can I Tell You? Secrecy and Disclosure with Children When a Family Member Has AIDS. Drawing on the experiences of families and professionals, this book explores the complex and diverse issues that surround the disclosure of the HIV diagnosis to children. [By Mary Tasker; ACCH, 1992. To order: 7910 Woodmont Avenue, Suite 300, Bethesda, MD 20814; 301/654-6549.]

■ DEATH AND DYING

Lifetimes provides a very simple explanation of living and dying, suitable to read with very young children. It is a beautiful way to explain death to children. [By Bryan Mellonie and Robert Ingpen; Bantam Books, 1983. To order: 2451 S. Wolf Rd., Des Plaines, IL 60018; 800/323-9872.]

About Dying, an open book for parents and children together, is a clearly told story of a little boy's bereavement. The book has large print and photographs for children throughout and small print for adults. [By Sara Bonnett Stein and Dick Frank; Walker and Co., 1974. To order: 720 5th Avenue, New York, NY 10019; 800/289-2553.]

When Death Walks In is a book for teenagers who have lost someone special. It is an excellent, clearly written resource for teens and adults that deals with all the feelings that may be part of grief. [By Mark Scrivani; Centering Corporation, 1991. To order: 1513 N. Saddle Creek Rd., Omaha, NE 68104; 402/553-1200.]

How Do We Tell the Children? A Parent's Guide to Helping Children Understand and Cope When Someone Dies is a step-by-step guide to talking about death with children aged two through the teens. Valuable for families, educators, and family-care professionals, this book includes a unique crisis intervention guide as well as sample "scripts" to help in explaining death. [By Dan Schaefer and Christine Lyons; Newmarket Press, 1988. To order: 18 East 48th St., New York, NY 10017; 800-726-0600.]

Talking About Death: A Dialogue Between Parent and Child is a compassionate guide for adults and children to read together, featuring a read-along story, answers to questions children ask about death, and a comprehensive list of helpful resources and organizations. [By E. Grollman; Beacon Press, 1991. To order: 25 Beacon St., Boston, MA 02108; 800-788-6262.]

After You Say Goodbye: When Someone You Love Dies of AIDS explores the grieving process and the special problems and needs associated with an AIDS-related loss. [By Paul Kent Forman; Chronicle Books, 1992. To order: Chronicle Books, 275 Fifth St., San Francisco, CA 94103; 800-722-6657.]

■ SEPARATION, LOSS, AND CHANGE

Changing Families: A Guide for Kids and Grown-ups is a workbook for kids experiencing divorce and separation. The chapters on feelings, building new families, and helping yourself have universal application. [By David Fassler, M.D., Michele Lash, and Sally B. Ives; Waterfront Books, 1988. To order: Talman Co., 131 Spring St., Suite 201E-N, New York, NY 10012; 800/537-8894.]

When Someone Has a Very Serious Illness is a wonderful workbook to help children learn to cope with any kind of serious (perhaps terminal) illness, and with loss and change. [By Marge Heegard; Woodland Press, 1991. To order: 99 Woodland Circle, Minneapolis, MN 55424; 612/926-2665.]

A Child's Journey through Placement is an excellent resource for child-helping professionals (social workers, therapists, juvenile justice workers) and parents (biological, foster, and adoptive) to support children who are separated from their families and in out-of-home care. It explains such concepts as attachment and separation, child development, separation and loss, and case planning. [By Vera Fahlberg, 1991. To order: Perspectives Press, P.O. Box 90318, Indianapolis, IN 46290-0318.]

■ OTHER ILLNESSES

It Helps to Have Friends is a free booklet especially useful for preadolescents and teens whose parents have cancer. [Produced by the American Cancer Society, 1987. Call 800/ACS-2345. Free.]

Back To School is a free handbook for parents of children with cancer, and is practical for parents of children coping with any serious illness. [Produced by the American Cancer Society, 1988. Call 800/ACS-2345. Free.]

The Happy Grandpa Has Heart Trouble is a storybook that explains heart attack and coronary bypass surgery, and ends happily. [By Jack Button, 1989; The Washington Hospital Center. To order: contact the Office of Public Affairs and Marketing; 202/877-6301.]

■ ADOPTION AND FOSTER CARE

Zachary's New Home is a brief but useful story for foster and adoptive parents and their children, using the story of a kitten cared for by two geese. [By Geraldine and Paul Blomquist; Magination Press, 1994. To order: 19 Union Square W., 8th Floor, NY, NY 10003; 212/924-3344.]

Being Adopted, written in a child's words, is an excellent resource for young children who cannot remember their biological parents, as well as for those have experienced or will soon experience separation from those they love and join with a new loving and caring family. [By Stephanie Herbert; CWLA, 1993. To order: CWLA c/o CSCC, PO Box 7816, 300 Raritan Center Parkway, Edison, NJ 08818; 908/225-1900.]

I Miss My Foster Parents is a wonderful account of the fear and anxiety children feel when they must leave the only home they know to begin a new life with a new family. [By Stefon Herbert; CWLA, 1993. To order: CWLA c/o CSCC, PO Box 7816, 300 Raritan Center Parkway, Edison, NJ 08818; 908/225-1900.]

The Visit details a child's feelings when she is separated from her brothers and sisters and describes one child's excitement in preparing for a visit with her siblings. [By S. Latisha Herbert; CWLA, 1993. To order: CWLA c/o CSCC, PO Box 7816, 300 Raritan Center Parkway, Edison, NJ 08818; 908/225-1900.]

My Foster Family is a coloring book that offers children ages five through 11 entering family foster care the opportunity to explore their feelings. It provides a gentle and thoughtful description of both the logistical and emotional changes that a young child entering a new home environment is likely to face. [By Jennifer Levine; CWLA, 1994. To order: CWLA c/o CSCC, PO Box 7816, 300 Raritan Center Parkway, Edison, NJ 08818; 908/225-1900.]

Because You Love Them: A Parent's Planning Guide is a workbook to help parents who have HIV disease or other illnesses plan for their children's future. It provides information on such topics as exploring family members' feelings about the illness; telling children, family members and friends about the illness; selecting future caregivers for children; accessing the range of financial services and support services that are needed for planning; and providing children with a family history. [By Lisa Merkel-Holguín, 1994. To order: CDC National AIDS Clearinghouse; 800/458-5231.]

■ OTHER

Orphans of the HIV Epidemic: Unmet Needs in Six U.S. Cities explores the national problem of the HIV epidemic in terms of the unmet needs of HIV-affected youth. The authors outline recommendations in a variety of areas: social services, training and professional development, public policy, legal standards, and further research needs. [By Carol Levine and Gary Stein, 1994. To order: The Orphan Project, 121 Avenue of the Americas, 6th Floor, New York, NY 10013; 212-925-5290.]

Who Will Take Care of Me? A Manual for Parents with HIV/AIDS outlines for parents who are HIV infected some necessary steps in establishing a plan for their children's future. [By the New York Council on Adoptable Children, 1993. To order: 666 Broadway, New York, NY 10012; 212/475-0222.]

Who Will Take Care of Me? A Manual for Professionals Working with Children Whose Parents Have HIV/AIDS surveys the key issues with which professionals must be familiar in order to provide support to parents living with HIV/AIDS who are making permanency plans for their children. [By the New York Council on Adoptable Children, 1993. To order: 666 Broadway, New York, NY 10012; 212/475-0222.]

Forgotten Children of the AIDS Epidemic, written by a diverse group of professionals, is a comprehensive guidebook that examines the issues facing children whose parents or siblings are infected with HIV/AIDS. Complete with a resource directory, action agenda, and personal stories, this book is a useful reference for policymakers, community workers, and families. [Edited by Shelley Geballe, Janice Gruendel, and Warren

Andiman, 1995. To order: Order Department, Yale University Press, P.O. Box 209040, New Haven, CT 06520-9040; 800/987-7323.]

Second Family Program: One Model for Permanency Planning with HIV-Affected Families is an excellent technical manual that describes the philosophy, development and planning processes, project components, staff training, and the recruitment of second families in this innovative program. [By Cathy Blanford, Phyllis Charles, and Sally Mason. To order: Lutheran Social Services of Illinois, 6525 West North Avenue, Suite 212, Oak Park, IL 60302; 708/445-8341.]

■ OTHER REFERENCES (NOT ANNOTATED)

Blake, J. (1990). *Risky times: How to be AIDS-smart and stay healthy: A guide for teenagers.* New York: Workman Publishing.

Glasser, E., and Palmer, L. (1991). *In the absence of angels.* New York: The Berkeley Publishing Group.

Johnson, A. (1993). *A rock and a hard place: One boy's triumphant story.* New York: Penguin Group.

Johnson, E. (1992). *What you can do to avoid AIDS.* New York: Times Books, Random House.

Lomax, G., and Sandler, J. (1988). Psychotherapy and consultation with persons with AIDS, *Psychiatric Annals, 18*, 4.

Novotny, P. (1991). *What women should know about chronic infections and sexually transmitted diseases.* New York: Dell Publishing.

Pastore, J. (Ed.). (1993). *Confronting AIDS through literature: The responsibilities of representation.* Urbana, IL: University of Illinois Press.

Peabody, B. (1986). *The screaming room: A mother's journal of her son's struggle with AIDS— A true story of love, devotion, and courage.* New York: Avon Books.

Pearson, C. (1988). *Goodbye, I love you.* New York: The Berkeley Publishing Group.

Quackenbuch, M., Nelson, M., and Clark, K. (Eds.) (1988). *The AIDS challenge: Prevention education for young people.* Santa Cruz, CA: Network Publications.

Reamer, F. (Ed.) (1991). *AIDS and Ethics.* New York: Columbia University Press.

Soler, M. Shotton, A., and Bell, J. (1993). *Glass walls: Confidentiality provisions and interagency collaborations.* San Francisco: Youth Law Center.

White, R., and Cunningham, A. (1992). *My own story.* New York: Penguin Books.

Winiarski, M. (1991). *AIDS-related psychotherapy.* Elmsford, NY: Pergamon Press.

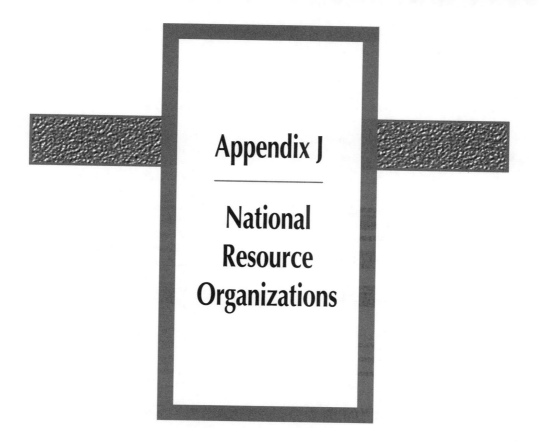

Appendix J

National Resource Organizations

■ NATIONAL HOTLINES

These AIDS Hotlines offer educational information concerning HIV/AIDS. Skilled information specialists answer questions, distribute written materials, and refer persons to other organizations.

AIDS Hotline for the Hearing Impaired
800-243-7889 (TDD Phone Line)

CDC AIDS Statistical Information Hotline
(for updated statistics on HIV/AIDS)
404/332-4570

CDC AIDS
Fax Information Service (a fax service that sends updated stats on HIV/AIDS)
404/332-4565

Gay/Lesbian Hotline
800/347-8336
Thursdays through Saturdays, 7pm-11:45pm EST

National AIDS Hotline
800/342-AIDS

National Native American AIDS Prevention Center
National Toll-Free AIDS Information Hotline
800/283-2437

National Pediatric AIDS Hotline
800/362-0071

National Social Security Hotline
(for information and assistance on many Social Security programs)
800/772-1213

Spanish AIDS Hotline
800/344-SIDA

■ NATIONAL CLEARINGHOUSES AND RESOURCE CENTERS

ARCH (Access to Respite Care and Help) National Resource Center

800 Eastowne Drive, Suite 105
Chapel Hill, NC 27514
800/473-1727
Provides referrals, information, training, technical assistance, evaluation, and research activities on respite care to service providers, families, and states.

CDC National AIDS Information Clearinghouse

P.O. Box 6003
Rockville, MD 20849-6003
800/458-5231
The National AIDS Information Clearinghouse is the center of CDC's comprehensive reference referral and publications distribution service on AIDS information. The clearinghouse staff, along with national, regional, state, and local organizations, develop and deliver HIV prevention programs and services.

National Adoption Information Clearinghouse (NAIC)

11426 Rockville Pike, Suite 410
Rockville, MD 20852
301/231-6512
NAIC provides information on the adoption of children who are HIV affected and/or infected. NAIC annually responds to 6,000 general requests for information from adoption professionals, adoptive parents, biological parents, students, and others.

National Pediatric HIV Resource Center

15 South 9th Street
Newark, NJ 07107
201/268-8251
800/362-0071
The National Pediatric HIV Resource Center offers a range of services to professionals who serve care providers of children infected with HIV/AIDS. The center provides consultation, technical assistance, and training and serves as a forum for exploring public policy issues relating to the care of children, youths, and families with HIV infection.

National Resource Center on Permanency Planning

Hunter College School of Social Work
129 East 79th Street, Room 801
New York, NY 10021
212/452-7053
The two objectives of the National Resource Center on Permanency Planning are to: 1) discover, document, and disseminate knowledge of permanency planning practice and exemplary programs; and 2) collaborate with other agencies across the United States to build knowledge in challenging areas and build agency capacity to meet these challenges through training and education, technical assistance, and model program development. This center has expertise in permanency planning and HIV/AIDS.

AIDS Clinical Trial Information Service (ACTIS)

National Institutes of Health, AIDS Prevention
800-TRIALS-A (874-2572)
Monday-Friday, 9am-7pm EST
ACTIS is a central service providing current information on federally and privately sponsored clinical trials for persons with AIDS and other people infected with HIV, including medical trials and therapy information.

■ NATIONAL ORGANIZATIONS: CHILDREN AND FAMILIES AND HIV/AIDS

Child Welfare League of America

440 First Street, NW, Suite 310
Washington, DC 20001-2085
202/638-2952
The Child Welfare League of America (CWLA) is a national, nonprofit membership association of more than 800 public and private nonprofit child welfare agencies throughout the 50 states and Canada. Since 1987, CWLA has worked to prepare and assist child welfare agencies to care for children, youths, and families affected by HIV/AIDS. CWLA has developed a series of guidelines and training materials for child welfare agencies. The materials listed below can be purchased from CWLA's Distribution Center by calling 908/225-1900.

CWLA Books

■ *Because You Love Them: A Parent's Planning Guide* (1994)

■ *Serving Children with HIV Infection in Child Day Care: A Guide for Center-Based and Family Day Care Providers* (1991)

■ *Meeting the Challenge of HIV Infection in Family Foster Care* (1991)

■ *Serving HIV-Infected Children, Youths, and their Families: A Guide for Residential Group Care Providers* (1989)

■ *Report of the CWLA Task Force on Children and AIDS: Initial Guidelines* (1988)

CWLA Curricula and Videos

■ *The Hugs InVited Education and Training Series* includes discussion guides and the following four videos: *Caring for Infants and Toddlers with HIV Infection; Caring for School-aged Children with HIV Infection; Adolescents—At Risk for HIV Infection; and Living with Loss— Children and HIV* (1991).

■ Project Champ materials, which include *Caring at Home: A Guide for Families,* and *Caring in the Community for Children with HIV: A Training Guide for Child Care Providers, Foster Families, Home Health Aides, and Volunteers.* (1991)

■ *With Loving Arms:* portrays three foster families caring for children who are HIV infected. (1989)

Children with AIDS Project of America

PO Box 83131
Phoenix, AZ 85071-3131
800/866-2437
The Children with AIDS Project of America recruits and provides services for adoptive, foster, and biological parents of children with HIV/AIDS and healthy children of parents with HIV/AIDS.

Foundation for Children with AIDS

1800 Columbus Avenue
Boston, MA 02119
617/442-7442
The Foundation for Children with AIDS is a national, nonprofit foundation that disseminates information on HIV/AIDS, and operates two programs: Project STAR, a pilot direct service project for preschool children who have HIV or who have a sibling with HIV; and the Kinship Project, a family-based program for families with preschool children affected by substance abuse. The Foundation also has a training center for AIDS-related issues, issues of substance abuse, family-centered care, and transagency case management.

Institute for Family-Centered Care

5715 Bent Branch Road
Bethesda, MD 20816
301/320-2686
The Institute for Family-Centered Care works with families and professionals to promote family-centered care for children with special needs. The Institute coordinates a national network of families and caregivers of children with HIV/AIDS.

National Network for Runaway and Youth Services

Safe Choices Project
1319 F Street NW, Suite 401
Washington, DC 20004
202/783-7949
Through its Safe Choices Project, the National Network for Runaway and Youth Services provides HIV/AIDS-related prevention materials, training, and technical assistance to shelters and programs serving runaway youths, homeless youths, and other youths in high-risk situations. In addition, the project informs national organizations and public decision makers about HIV and young people in high-risk situations. The project is also expanding its efforts to provide materials and technical assistance on issues related to lesbian, gay, and bisexual youth. The National Network's Safe Choices Technical Assistance Hotline [800/878-AIDS] provides help in developing programs or finding new HIV/AIDS related materials.

Pediatric AIDS Foundation

1311 Colorado Avenue
Santa Monica, CA 90404
310/395-9051
The Pediatric AIDS Foundation provides education programs for parents, conducts research on perinatal HIV transmission, supplies hospitals serving pediatric AIDS populations with funds to address unmet needs, and funds interns working in pediatric AIDS.

■ OTHER NATIONAL AIDS RESOURCES

AIDS Action Council

1875 Connecticut Avenue NW, Suite 700
Washington, DC 20009
202/986-1300
The AIDS Action Council is the only national
organization devoted solely to advocating at the
federal level for more effective AIDS policy, legislation, and funding. The council represents more
than 1,000 community-based AIDS service organizations throughout the United States.

AIDS National Interfaith Network

110 Maryland Avenue NE, Suite 504
Washington, DC 20002
800/288-9619
The AIDS National Interfaith Network provides
referrals to more than 2,000 local and regional
AIDS ministries for people in different faith communities (Christian, Unitarian, and Jewish).

American Association for World Health
(AAWH)

1129 20th Street NW, Suite 400
Washington, DC 20036
202/ 466-5883
AAWH is an educational and charitable non-
governmental membership organization. Its purpose is to inform the public about major health
challenges that affect people both nationally and
internationally and to promote cooperative solutions that emphasize grassroots involvement.
AAWH works with a variety of health organizations and individuals throughout the United
States, including the World Health Organization
and the Pan American Health Organization.

American Red Cross

Office of HIV Education
1750 K Street NW, Suite 700
Washington, DC 20006
202/973-6002
The Office of HIV Education provides four sets of
materials and training for different ages and ethnic
groups in order to prepare instructors. These include
the HIV/AIDS Instructors' Course, the African
American HIV/AIDS Program, the Hispanic
HIV/AIDS Program, and the HIV/AIDS in the
Workplace Program. The office also provides a large
range of teaching materials in English and Spanish,
which are available from local Red Cross chapters.

Center for Women Policy Studies

National Resource Center on Women and AIDS
2000 P Street NW, Suite 508
Washington, DC 20036
202/872-1770
The National Resource Center on Women and
AIDS addresses critical policy issues for women
and HIV. It is a centralized resource for researchers,
advocates, care providers, and policymakers seeking
information on women and AIDS. The Center
defines key policy issues and develops strategies to
place these issues on the federal policy agenda.

Hispanic AIDS Forum

121 Avenue of the Americas, Suite 505
New York, NY 10013
212/966-6336
The Hispanic AIDS Forum keeps the Hispanic
community involved and aware of AIDS by working on both citywide and community levels in the
areas of public policy, advocacy, communications,
research, education, and support services to combat the epidemic.

National Association of People with AIDS

1413 K Street NW, 8th Floor
Washington, DC 20005
202/898-0414
The National Association of People with AIDS
(NAPWA) serves as a voice for people with
HIV/AIDS, and has an information and referral
service, advocacy program, educational service,
publications, and a national speakers bureau.

National Association of Social Workers
(NASW)

750 First Street, NE
Washington, DC 20002
202/408-8600
800/638-8799, ext. 444 (Help Desk)
NASW provides continuing education programs
on HIV/AIDS at both state and national conferences, publishes articles within several journals
such as *Social Work* and *Health and Social Work*,
provides a network of HIV/AIDS liaisons who can
be contacted through the state chapter office, and
has issued a national policy statement on
HIV/AIDS, which can be obtained through the
NASW Help Desk.

National Association of State Boards of Education (NASBE)

1012 Cameron Street
Alexandria, VA 22314
703/684-4000

NASBE tracks the development of school policies relating to HIV at the state level and provides assistance and advice to educators and policymakers on school health and HIV-related policies.

National Conference of State Legislatures

HIV/AIDS Project
1560 Broadway, Suite 700
Denver, CO 80202
303/830-2200

The HIV/AIDS Project, funded by the CDC, monitors and shares HIV/AIDS policy information with state legislatures. The project serves as an information clearinghouse, and provides in-depth state technical assistance, facilitates dialogue between legislatures and public health officials, sponsors annual meetings, and provides publications on HIV/AIDS related issues.

National Hospice Organization

1901 North Moore Street, Suite 901
Arlington, VA 22209
800/658-8898.

The National Hospice Organization provides information on and referrals for hospice care.

National Institutes of Health

Department of Allergy and Infectious Diseases
Building 31, Room 7A50
9000 Rockville Pike
Bethesda, MD 20892
301/496-5717

The Allergy and Infectious Disease Department performs biomedical research and produces pamphlets on allergies and infectious diseases, including HIV/AIDS, to assist patients.

National Leadership Coalition on AIDS

1730 M Street NW, Suite 905
Washington, DC 20036
202/429-0930

The goal of the National Leadership Coalition on AIDS is to marshall the collective resources of business and labor to prevent and combat the spread of HIV. It provides information on HIV/AIDS policy and education in the workplace.

National Minority AIDS Council (NMAC)

300 I Street NE, Suite 400
Washington, DC 20002
202/544-1076
800/669-5052

NMAC provides minority organizations with resources to fight the AIDS epidemic and to protect families, including technical assistance programs; public policy initiatives; and outreach, education, care, housing, and support services targeted to assist minority community-based organizations responding to HIV/AIDS.

National Native American AIDS Prevention Center

3515 Grand Avenue, Suite 100
Oakland, CA 94610
510/444-2051

The National Native American AIDS Prevention Center conducts outreach to native organizations and communities, trains community-based HIV educators, and provides technical assistance to community organizations. It operates the National Toll-Free Aids Information Line, the National Information Clearinghouse for Native-specific AIDS information, a quarterly newsletter called *Seasons,* and a circular for target populations.

About the
Author

Lisa Merkel-Holguín spearheaded CWLA's HIV/AIDS initiative from mid 1993 to early 1995. In that capacity, she developed these guidelines, with assistance from the CWLA Task Force on Children and HIV Infection. These guidelines are a companion piece to another work by the author entitled *Because You Love Them: A Parent's Planning Guide*—a book that some have called the most powerful, compassionate, and useful resource that assists parents living with HIV/AIDS in planning for their children's future. As the HIV/AIDS Program Manager at CWLA, she developed other program and policy statements, served as a public speaker, and wrote numerous grants.

In addition, Ms. Merkel-Holguín has other published works in such areas as child welfare statistics and outcome measures. She received her MSW from the University of Illinois at Urbana-Champaign. She now works as a Program/Policy Analyst for the Children's Division of the American Humane Association in Englewood, CO.